What Dreams Are (Not Quite) Made Of

No fame, no fortune, just football... and Multiple Sclerosis

Tom Youngs

Vertical Editions
www.verticaleditions.com

First published in the United Kingdom in 2016 by Vertical Editions, Unit 4a,
Snaygill Industrial Estate, Skipton, North Yorkshire BD23 2QR

www.verticaleditions.com

ISBN 978-1-904091-96-7

A CIP catalogue record for this book is available from the British Library

Cover design by HBA, York

Printed and bound by Jellyfish Print Solutions, Swanmore, Hants

For Chelle, Hannah and Orla,
who make everything worthwhile

Contents

Acknowledgements

"A footballer, hey? What was that like?" This book is part my attempt at answering that question – the one most asked of me whenever I meet somebody new – and part an effort to encourage a bit more openness and understanding about Multiple Sclerosis. Whether or not I am able to achieve those aims, I'd like to thank a few people for at least helping me to get the opportunity.

Firstly, thanks to Lawrie Madden, my former tutor at Staffordshire University, who guided me on my way to a first-class degree in sports writing, and then, after hearing my germ of a book idea, put me in touch with Nick Johnson. Nick, head of media at Chesterfield FC and co-author of Mel Sterland's autobiography, gave me invaluable tips and advice on my early draft chapters and also recommended Vertical Editions as a publisher worth approaching.

They certainly were worth it. Karl Waddicor has been so encouraging and helpful throughout the whole process, which has ended up far less stressful than I might have anticipated as a first-time author. I'm very grateful for that. I'd also like to mention Ian Bayley and Dave Watters. Ian was my feature writing tutor at university and Dave was my editor at *Non-League Today* – both gave me a lot of confidence in my ability to write effectively and without them this book would not exist.

Less direct but no less inspirational influences can be found in the football autobiographies of Graeme Le Saux, Paul Lake and, with an eye on the under-represented lower leagues, Garry Nelson and Eamon Dunphy. And speaking of other footballers, I have to thank my former team-mates, coaches and managers at all levels – even those I didn't often agree with – for contributing so richly to my career and to this story.

Finally, the biggest appreciation must go to two people. Mum, whose selflessness and unstinting support were key to my realising the dream of becoming a professional footballer and have never relented since. And Chelle, my wife, for being – cliché alert – my rock throughout the ups and downs of my career, for giving me two wonderful children and for dealing so positively with the more challenging times of the last five years. And also for playing the vital role of primary sub-editor, fact checker and memory aid once I'd finished the first draft of the book.

1

MS and the
Undercover Footballer

There's never an easy way to have to give up football. But this wasn't what I was expecting.

It started at Boots Opticians in Bury St Edmunds. "I'm terribly sorry, Mr Youngs," began the ophthalmologist. "I'm a bit puzzled. I can't find anything wrong with your eye. It looks perfectly healthy to me." I had just failed miserably to identify, with my left eye, any of the letters – even the biggest ones – on an eye chart a few feet away. My eye certainly didn't seem perfectly healthy.

I'd phoned up for an appointment a couple of days previously when I realised I was struggling to see my computer screen properly at work. I thought maybe I'd damaged the eye somehow, that it had become misshapen. An astigmatism, or something like that. I was fully prepared to be told I needed glasses. I wasn't particularly bothered about it. Heck, work would probably even contribute to the cost.

But I was less prepared for the slew of sight tests and eye examinations to leave the expert at a loss. Now I was worried. If my eye was perfectly healthy, why on earth couldn't I see anything through it other than a hazy wash of indistinct colours? I was referred to hospital, where I was the youngest patient in the eye clinic waiting room by a considerable margin. Cataracts were the order of the day. I was prescribed some eye drops to reduce inflammation and irritation, and asked to return in a couple of weeks if my symptoms did not improve.

They did not.

This time I saw a different doctor, who within seconds seemed a lot more confident of what he was dealing with. "You see that?" he asked the trainee alongside him as he waved a torch across my eye-line. "You are suffering from optic neuritis," he advised me. "As we are now six weeks from when the symptoms started, it looks like it may not be going away. Have a look on the internet to see what that might mean, and we'll pencil you back in for an appointment in a month to see if there are any changes."

I called my wife on the way back to the office and within seconds her smartphone informed us that optic neuritis is often a presenting sign of multiple sclerosis, the central nervous system disorder. As Chelle reeled off a bunch of other MS symptoms, a further one caught my attention. "'Lhermitte's sign'," she said, "is an electrical sensation that shoots down the back and into the limbs." That was the clincher. Pretty much every time I'd got out of my chair at work in recent months, I had experienced what felt like an electric shock coursing down my back and sides. I'd put it down to sleeping in an awkward position, but now it seemed clear what was actually going on. Having to wear glasses certainly would have been preferable.

I could tell on the phone that Chelle was immediately fraught with worry. Like me, she didn't really know what MS was, so her mind was racing through possible outcomes, mistaking it – in the heat of the moment – for everything from Motor Neurone Disease to brain tumours. All with our two-week-old second daughter awaiting a nappy change on the floor of the living room. I tried to calm Chelle down, asking her to wait until I'd been back for my follow-up, but I knew she would, understandably, find it hard. She was scared. Of what the future might entail for us and our young family. And, while I tried to stay as composed and rational as possible, I was scared too.

I knew next to nothing about MS. I vaguely remembered that a friend's mum suffered from it, and that it didn't seem to treat her too well, but it wasn't a condition that had impacted anyone close to me. So I wasn't sure what to expect as I was passed on to the neurology department at the hospital, who sent me for an MRI scan. When I came in for my results, Dr Molyneux pulled the screen round to show me the cross-sections of my brain. "If you look here," he explained, "you can see some small lesions; pockets of inflammation which are consistent with the issues you have been experiencing."

Suddenly, the whole episode became a bit more real at this point. Seeing a picture of some defects on your brain will do that. A disorder of the nervous system sounds a bit more abstract, less tangible, not so clear-cut. Cloudy patches on your brain hits things home. It was quite a shock.

I thought I was done with hospital shocks three years before, when prominent hip specialist Sam Parsons laid bare the reasons that I was struggling to regain mobility after a heavy fall on the pitch. "These x-rays look more like I would expect from someone in their seventies," he said as he outlined the severity of my advanced osteo-arthritis. "If you get past 40 without coming back to me for a double hip replacement, I'll buy you a pint." I was 32.

But as shocking as that was at the time, bringing an abrupt end to my (by now firmly *semi*-professional) playing career, it's easier to process a physical issue like that. If I avoided activities that would put my hips under pressure, I felt I could manage the pain and the problem and delay the need for surgery. It seemed straightforward.

It seemed a lot less straightforward to stop lesions emerging in your brain, especially when no-one can be sure what caused them to be there in the first place. Indeed, after a lumbar puncture test provided further evidence of probable MS, a follow-up MRI scan confirmed the development of additional lesions. Dr Molyneux could now firmly diagnose what I had been pretty sure of since that torch test a year previously.

But, even then, it wasn't as if the doctor could give me any clear idea of what lay ahead. Although my visual problems had calmed down to some extent, there had been quite a few more good indicators in the time it took for the diagnosis to be verified. My legs or feet would sometimes go to sleep if I was in the same position for too long, and could stay numb for quite some time. Episodes of chronic itching would come, furiously, and then disappear without reason or treatment. My legs would sometimes buckle, as if someone was twanging the nerves behind my knees, and I also developed a nasty habit of tripping when walking up stairs. My foot just seemed not to lift as high as I expected it to.

As MS is so enigmatic, though, it's difficult to say categorically that it caused all, or indeed any, of these symptoms. They were all new to me, so it seemed the most likely explanation, but the doctor couldn't be sure as they were relatively minor complaints. That was the most difficult thing with the diagnosis, the not knowing. The doctor had seen patients who were confined to a wheelchair, but also some whose symptoms had barely developed beyond the first attack. What my path would be, he could not say. I read about a man who lived for 13 years after his diagnosis with almost no ill effects, then within two months was struggling to walk and unable to work. The prospect of that sudden deterioration from healthy to drastically impaired was – and remains – frightening.

At this point, though, the biggest effect on me – one which the doctor *was* confident of putting down to the disease – was not very visible to those around me. It was tiredness.

I've never been someone who needs a lot of sleep. During my professional playing days, I would often only sleep for three or four hours a night during the close season, without a day's training to wear me out. After my MS symptoms began, though, I would sometimes drop off in the early evening, or on a weekend afternoon, or even while reading my little girls a bedtime story. This was unprecedented for me, and it would come out of nowhere, as if Derren Brown had secretly popped in to hypnotise me.

As the 2013/14 season drew to a close, my role as assistant manager (formerly player-assistant, until the hips gave way) at my hometown club, Mildenhall Town, was leaving me drained and run down. With work and family commitments non-negotiable, I just had too much on my plate. Nothing particularly debilitating had hit me yet, but I felt I needed my body and mind at their strongest to keep the condition at bay.

Football had to go.

It was a sad day when I realised this was my only real option, just like it had been when Mr Parsons told me I would never play again. But, as then, I tried to avoid mourning a loss, preferring instead to be thankful that I had ever been able to join the words 'football' and 'career' in a meaningful sentence – a fleetingly-held dream for most men. Given that my hips had clearly been a ticking, hereditary time-bomb for a while, and that MS is known to present at any time between 20 and 40, I was very fortunate that both problems lay dormant long enough to allow me 18 years of involvement in the adult game, including ten as a full-time professional.

Although, in truth, for much of those ten years I did feel somewhat like an undercover agent trying to avoid being unmasked in a world for which I was unsuited. Not in terms of my merits as a footballer – although every player at every level, no matter how deep their well of self-belief, goes through crises of confidence from time to time – but in terms of my membership in football's cult: the dressing room.

There seems to be almost a legal requirement for ex-players to say "what I miss is the dressing room", or something similar, when asked about how they are dealing with their exit from the profession. I find it hard to share that view. What I miss is playing football for a living. The best job in the world. Not anything else, though.

Please don't get me wrong. I fully realise the possibility of coming across as a bitter has-been having a snipe at the game, the wannabe superstar who never made it big (of which there are plenty about). That's not me. Yes, I spent my ten years as a professional exclusively in the third and fourth tiers of English football, and yes, I wish I could have played higher. But, ultimately, I wasn't good enough. The game moved on so much in terms of physicality and athleticism in the early years of my career, I was left behind, and I wasn't technically outstanding enough to compensate for my deficiencies. It wasn't for lack of effort, attitude or application, though. I was a dedicated professional, so I'm at peace with what I was and was not able to achieve in the game.

And I got on really well with many of my colleagues in the various dressing rooms I was a part of. I shared lots of happy times with them. Lots of laughter. I'll never pretend that I didn't enjoy myself immensely at times. But, as all my former team-mates would no doubt testify, I wasn't exactly a standard fit for the dressing room environment. My various nicknames, aside from Youngsie, all shared a similar theme. The Professor, Boffin, Statto, DangerStat (a cunning combination of Danger Mouse – for my looks – and Statto) and Tory Boy (for being like a public schoolboy rather than for any political persuasion).

Clearly it was acknowledged that I wasn't 'one of the lads', at least in the stereotypical sense. Laddish I certainly am not. I'm not into cars. Or driving them fast. I don't like golf. Or bragging about my sexual conquests (even if I'd had any to brag about). Or pretty much anything that is likely to pop up in dressing room conversation very often.

Asked once what I'd got for my birthday, I revealed the *Select* music magazine to which I'd been newly subscribed. A couple of the lads gamely flicked through it, but the only thing that briefly piqued their interest was a picture which had them wondering whether Placebo frontman Brian Molko was "a bloke or a bird". Obviously there was a lack of bare female flesh compared to the copies of *Loaded* and *FHM* dotted around.

Not being 'blokey' in the most 'blokey' of climates wasn't in itself the issue, though. In any walk of life some people have different interests, different demeanours and different senses of humour. Some of the dressing room 'banter' I found banal and juvenile – hardly a surprise when you rip teenage boys straight out of school and cocoon them in a sheltered, insular, competitive world which is essentially an extension of the playground – but some of it was uproariously funny. Even for a bookish, nerdy liberal like me.

And though I was generally pretty quiet, I always made sure I said enough to fit in. My geeky reputation attracted enough attention to let me in on the lifeblood of the dressing room: the piss-take. You have to give and take a bit of stick to truly belong, and that wasn't a problem. So I would never cast myself as a complete fish out of water. But there were two elements of the dressing room exchanges that left me deeply uncomfortable.

The first was an unabashed, unbridled prejudice that played a large part in the piss-take. Openly gay footballers (at least ones who come out before retirement) have remained conspicuous by their absence, and if you spent half an hour in a dressing room you would realise why. Gay this. Queer that. Poof this. Bender that. Any failing on the football pitch could be equated to being gay.

Less than progressive attitudes towards homosexuality are certainly not the preserve of footballers. They are very probably present in every workplace in the country to some extent. But in other arenas they are governed and curbed far more by political correctness and discrimination law. Of course, technically the latter applies in a dressing room as well, but who would demand that it is adhered to?

Who would want to make themselves such an outsider in a fragile job where the relationship with your team-mates can be key to your success? In a job where you might see a man in his thirties, with no sense of irony, flailing his genitals in front of an 18-year-old kid in order to catch his eye and proclaim *him* guilty of 'gay shit'. Clearly a heinous 'crime' in football's macho world. All just 'a bit of banter'. But imagine that teenager is actually gay, or still confused about his own sexuality. How would that make him feel? Comfortable and ready to excel on the training pitch the next day?

The chat then turns to what's on at the cinema. "That *Brokeback Mountain's* been getting great reviews," someone points out. "Yeah, but it's about *bummers*, isn't it?" comes a response. Cue guffaws and the sort of grunts of agreement you hear at Prime Minister's questions. And this is all before you even think about how fans might react.

My brother-in-law is gay, but I don't think that necessarily made me any more uncomfortable with the bigotry than I would naturally be. I just found it completely vulgar and distasteful. But it will only take one brave player to break the taboo and the floodgates will probably open. Rumours have suggested recently that it may even happen before this book is published. I really hope so, because if there was a young gay man in any of the dressing rooms I was part of – and often we were told, in 70s sitcom fashion, that statistically there must be at least one so we "should be careful" – it would have been a very difficult place to be. If an established and respected player did come out, it would probably draw a line under the issue immediately.

The other discomfiting element was not always displayed quite so blatantly, but was still ever-present. 'Kick Racism Out of Football' used to be emblazoned on our warm-up tops once a year to remind the public how much progress has been made in the game over the past 30 years or so. But while we've seen the back of monkey noises and bananas thrown onto the pitch, a more casual, sub-conscious prejudice is still very apparent in the dressing room. Even with so many black faces in our dressing rooms.

The black lads I played with were so accustomed to it, they didn't even care – or even laughed along – when questions such as "what would you do if your daughter brought big (*insert stereotypical black name – most settled on Leroy*) home with her?" floated across the dressing room. I remember our physio at Cambridge, Stuart Ayles, being left in total disbelief when someone – openly and shamelessly – asked him that particular one.

And the attitudes could be even more deplorable when the chat was more back-room, more hush-hush, in acknowledgement that any black colleague would be deeply offended if they overheard. Stereotypes (and ridiculous ones at that) ascribed to black players, using the terms 'they' or 'them'. 'They' always back each other up against the rest of the dressing room. 'They' don't dig in when things get tough.

But at least, with so many black players around, there was an appreciation that the attitude was not acceptable for a mass audience. With so few Asians in the game, there was no such suppression of the word 'paki'. It was happily bandied about. Once, when one of my team-mates came back for pre-season training with a particularly intense sun tan, he was even nicknamed 'Paki' for a few weeks. I was chuckled at for refusing to use the term if I joined in any conversation when others were doing so.

Of course, all of this could well be the same in any alpha male-dominated world. Building sites up and down the land may well be remarkably similar, for all I know. Blokes just being blokes, lads being lads. But, for me, the fabled dressing room was just a bit too narrow-minded, a bit too crowded with similar types. Which encouraged even the more moderate to join in, to be part of the team. And which made it difficult, nigh on impossible, to break from such ingrained prejudices. The type of 'institutionalised' bias that is often described when trying to explain why there are so few black coaches and managers.

And in a world where we're constantly told that English players are too one-dimensional compared to those from more exotic climes (though I think that's equally narrow-minded), I don't find that particularly healthy. People of all types and backgrounds should feel able to dream of becoming a footballer and not be put off by the intimidating air of ultra-masculinity, prejudice and perceived loutishness. Because if you can get past all of that, it really is the best job in the world.

I'm sure I wasn't the only one uncomfortable with some of the social aspects of dressing room life. And like the others, I just ignored what I didn't enjoy, dodged the conversations I didn't want to be a part of, and focused on the main event. For to earn a living by doing something that you would happily pay to do (like most players in the country do every weekend) is amazing. You spend a lot more time actually playing football than anything else, and I loved playing, whether on the training pitch or on a matchday. Whatever professional difficulties I had, be it disagreements with managers or losses of form, I could almost always find solace in that simple truth.

"Do you miss it?" seems to be the first thing most people say to me since I stepped away from the game. So do I? Not the dressing room. Not the 'banter'. But I will forever miss playing the game I love.

2

The Coldham's Common lottery

It was three weeks before Christmas, 1986, when I asked the question that shocked and delighted my dad in equal measure: "Do you think I could have a Tottenham shirt for Christmas please?"

In my first seven and a half years, I had shown next to no interest in football. Or pretty much any sport for that matter. Mildenhall Cricket Club – where my dad was a prominent player – was like a home from home, but while my younger brother Andrew was always out watching the game and picking up bats and balls, I was happiest in the clubhouse with a book or doing some colouring. I'd learnt to pledge allegiance to Spurs, parrot-fashion, when asked about it. But no more than that.

Mum always suspected that people would think my preference for more studious exploits came by her design, as she was a teacher. Utter nonsense, of course, but whatever the reasons behind it, it certainly came as a major surprise when I made my Christmas request, sparking a scramble to locate a stockist in double-quick time. But I got my shirt.

I'm not quite sure what drove my seemingly sudden fascination with football. Maybe it was a slow-burning excitement ignited by the previous summer's World Cup in Mexico, which I just about remember. It might have been a gradual realisation of how much Dad enjoyed the game, and wanting to be a part of that. Perhaps it was a desire to join in with the boys playing during lunch-break at school, whereas previously I think I was more into kiss-chase with the girls.

All of those could have been factors, but I actually think the roots of my transformation might have come from the same enthusiasm for books that had appeared to keep me away from sport. Dad had loads of football annuals and reference books from the sixties and seventies that I used to look through, and among them was a *Rothmans Football Yearbook*. I then remember being in WHSmith one day and seeing that there was a new one on the shelf. 1986/87. I was absolutely entranced by the mass of information inside. The previous season's results, appearances and goalscorers, the height and weight of the players, the club grounds and nicknames. I think I ended up getting that for Christmas as well.

From that festive period on, I was hooked. I have no recollection of the start of the 1986/87 season, but by the end of it I was crying in my bed as I listened on the radio to two late Arsenal goals winning a Littlewoods Cup semi-final replay at White Hart Lane. I was crying again when Dad took me to my first live game, the FA Cup Final, and Gary Mabbutt's knee diverted a cross over Ray Clemence's head to hand Coventry an unexpected Wembley triumph. Despite those tears, there was no turning back. Football was a part of me.

But as I began to play the game in scrappy lunchtime kickabouts at Great Heath Primary School, I had a lot of lost time to make up for. The popular myth is that some people are 'natural' footballers. That they are just born with an innate ability to play football. The reality is that while some inherited physical traits – pace, agility, balance – certainly offer an advantage and make it easier to get to grips with the game, the technical attributes and match awareness that mark out good players can only come from one thing: practice. And by the age of seven and a half, most of my football-mad friends had been playing the game in some form – even if it was just solo shooting against a wall – for a couple of years at least. Although on the school field I was soon one of the better players, it was mainly due to being quicker than everyone else, rather than any abundance of skill.

The next summer saw an under-nine team set up under the banner of Mildenhall Town. I joined straight away. To start with it was just weekly training, with a few friendly matches arranged with nearby Thetford. The matches tended to be hugely one-sided affairs, an 8-0 win for one side followed by a 7-0 victory for the other next time round. The first goal always seemed to be pretty crucial.

But while the matches were typical English schoolboy fare of the age – 11-a-side on a full-size pitch, kids freezing while they waited minutes to get another touch of the ball – it was the training over that first year that really helped me develop as a player. We were fortunate to have a coach in Andrew Neal ('Spider'), who was not only enthusiastic but knowledgeable, learning from the professional youth coaches he had seen to put on well-planned sessions that the boys could enjoy but also learn from.

Still, I wasn't much of a technician, though. I went to a summer football course with Sunshine Soccer, and one of the afternoons comprised of a keepy-ups competition. Everyone was allowed three attempts to post their best total. I'd always struggled with ball juggling and, though I'll admit to envying my friends who were good at it, I could never really understand what all the fuss was about. If I was on my own I would always practice kicking a ball against a wall and controlling the rebound in as few touches as possible to get a shot off. That's what I had to do in games, so I figured that's what I would do in practice. I think I managed 12 keepy-ups during my turn in the spotlight, while a few of the lads had to retire at 100 and got a share of the prize.

I did get an award on the course, though. It was a medal for 'best attitude'. It sounds like one of those prizes they give to kids who don't excel at the any of the actual skills, but it probably summed up where I was at that time. What I as yet lacked in ability, I made up for in effort and application.

By the 1988/89 season, Mildenhall were ready to join the Thetford & District Under-11 League. The games were now of a lot higher standard, although still on the huge pitches, with the huge goals which dwarfed 10-year-old goalkeepers and meant that if you could lift the ball five feet in the air – which I certainly couldn't – you were guaranteed to score. Although I think that sort of football is criminally bad for the development of nine and ten-year-olds – all any side needs is a big lad who can boot it a long way and at least one quick forward; the other nine players may as well watch planes fly over half the time – I must admit it felt great at the time to run out on the first-team pitch at Mildenhall. No matter how over-sized it was. It felt like a 'proper' game.

Unfortunately, many of the assorted parents and grandparents present used to treat it like a 'proper' game too, rather than a vehicle for their children to keep fit, have fun and learn a bit more about the game and themselves. So you had the frequent calls of "get stuck in", "take him out" or sometimes even more violent urgings from the touchline. "Get rid of it" and "get it forward" were also popular forms of encouragement. For my money, that is one of the most straightforward reasons why England teams have been perennial under-achievers, yet English football as a brand is the most popular in the world.

Whether or not you like to describe football as entertainment, ultimately that's what it is. People watch it to be entertained. And any entertainment has to fulfil the needs of its public. English fans like football played in a certain way. Fast. Frenetic. With plenty of tackles. And an emphasis on playing forward as much as possible. Even if there isn't an obvious reason to do so. We've all heard the groans when a player, not seeing a suitable forward option, plays it back into his own half. Or plays *another* square ball across the back. Patience is not always regarded as a virtue. It's the same whether you're talking about 75,000 packing out Old Trafford or 20 watching an under-11 match on a Sunday morning.

And as that is what English football fans want, that is what they get. Even when the Premier League now comes filled with largely foreign talent, who grew up in very different footballing cultures, the game is still played at breakneck pace with lots of early forward passes (even if crossing the ball now seems very out of fashion). It is really exciting. It's the game I fell in love with. And it's why our league is so marketable across the globe. It will always be thus because that is what is demanded by the spectators.

Even with the vast expenditure on academies, trying to

create a new generation of highly-skilled technical players, the first exposure to football kids get will be with parents watching who've grown up loving the English game for what it is. Fast and furious. Blood and thunder. And as those children grow up, no matter how technically gifted they are, every time they get in front of an English (or British) crowd – at any level, however far they go in the game – they will feel bound to play faster, play forward, be a bit more gung-ho, make more tackles. All those inappropriate shouts at my early games are just more evidence. It's how we like it. For 23 out of every 24 months. Then we moan when the rest of the world refuses to play the game our way in international tournaments and we lose.

Mildenhall's first season ended in a blaze of glory as we won the League (or Kevin Wilson) Cup, beating Thetford Panthers A 1-0 in the final thanks to an early tap-in from yours truly. We'd had a good campaign, competing well in most games even though more than half our team could still qualify as under-ten. But it was the start of the next season that proved pivotal in my nascent football 'career'.

In August, Spider took four or five of us along to an open trial for the Cambridge United centre of excellence. It took place on a rather dated astroturf pitch at Coldham's Common, just on the other side of the allotments which used to back on to United's ramshackle Abbey Stadium. The trial consisted of about 50 lads split into three small-sided games, with the teams rotating to face different opposition every 15 minutes or so.

I think there were only two coaches there, so it seemed a bit of a lottery; very much a case of hoping someone was watching when you had your good moments, and maybe not watching when you tripped over the ball. My touch had improved almost immeasurably over the past year or so, with all the additional training, but I was still at my best when given a ball to run on to so I could show a defender a clean pair of heels. The rather cramped format didn't play to my strengths, therefore, so I wasn't overly hopeful of being selected even though I did manage to score a few goals.

The only reason to be slightly more optimistic was the

presence of the coach Graham Scarff, who had taken a guest session at the Sunshine Soccer course a year earlier and appeared to remember me favourably from then. Sure enough, I got the nod, along with Spider's son Terry, and we were invited to come along to the Common every Monday evening for the rest of the season.

Graham – who also worked with the first team under John Beck – had such an infectious enthusiasm that he was a joy to work with. He was always clear and concise when making his coaching points, and had a way of criticising with humour that left you in no uncertain terms that you'd got something wrong, but engendered no fear of trying – and often failing – again.

At the end of the season the centre of excellence squad was taken to a tournament in Belgium. We were the only British side there, and were far too good for most of the opposition until a very close final, which we edged 1-0 thanks to a goal from my strike partner Andrew 'Porky' Claydon. Aside from some decent performances and a few goals which cemented me in the club's programme for another season, the most notable development for me on the tour was in terms of diet.

I was an extremely fussy eater and when I didn't like the look of the chicken salad our hosts had provided for one pre-match meal, I refused to eat it. There was some kind of sauce slathered on the chicken and potatoes, and I was way too suspicious of it to risk having a go. Fast forward a couple of hours and I was really struggling to get about the pitch as we played our final group game. Wilting in the heat, I somehow still managed to toe one past the goalkeeper to seal a 2-0 victory, but Scarffy was pretty scathing after the game. He'd noticed me fail to eat and hoped I had learnt a valuable lesson.

I had. And as I was gradually fed ever more dietary information throughout my time in youth football, I came to understand how important eating is in helping performance. Eating the right things and the right amount of them. It all served me well as I later made my way into the professional ranks, never allowing myself to be let down by poor pre-match eating. Not that I'm above being a bit fussy even now, mind. I'm still no huge fan of salad, though the odd green leaf is a more welcome addition to my plate. On occasion.

A few weeks after we returned home, I watched a few of my older team-mates from Belgium setting foot on the pitch at Wembley in the build-up to the national stadium's first ever play-off final, which Cambridge won 1-0 against Chesterfield. On the radio after the game, Scarffy name-checked me in saying what a fantastic year it had been for the club, "from Tiny Tom in the under-11s, right up to the first team." It was the beginning of something special for me and for the club.

A year later, the centre of excellence squad was taken back to the same tournament in Belgium. We listened to the radio in our room as news came through of the first team clinching the Third Division title, leapfrogging local rivals Southend on the final day of the season. And we sealed a second successive title in Belgium, with Tiny Tom bagging a hat-trick in the final (ok, the dubious goals panel might have stripped me of one of the goals had they been there, but in their absence I'm claiming a treble).

By the following year, as the first team narrowly missed out on promotion to the new Premier League, the centre of excellence set-up had changed beyond recognition. We now trained indoors at Bottisham Village College. Very few of the lads remained the same after further trials had seen most of them replaced by new blood. Graham was no longer involved, with much of the training being taken by Gary Johnson – John Beck's assistant with the first team – whose son Lee was in the ranks, a year younger than me.

I was extremely lucky to be a youngster at Cambridge in the early 1990s, with a succession of brilliant coaches to learn from. After Graham came Gary, under whom Gary Rowett – then a fledgling member of the first-team squad but more recently a bright young manager in charge of Birmingham City – would take sessions. Then came the Ashworth invasion: former Norwich trainee Paul – fresh from the success of his PASS soccer school – sometimes accompanied by his brother Dan (or Danny as we called him back then), last seen holding the entire future of English football in the palm of his hand as the FA's Director of Elite Development.

In football, and particularly as a striker, it's what might be called 'being in the right place at the right time'. But lots of people were in that same right place at the right time. The key was making the most of it.

In that respect, again I think that being a bit swottish was a huge advantage. Much as I'd always had a thirst for knowledge at school, so I had a desire to learn more about football. Being a Spurs fan, I absolutely idolised Gary Lineker. So I watched him religiously. But also read about him religiously. I was bought books that carried his name like *The Striker's Handbook* and *Striker: Skills and Tactics* and I would read every last word, study every last diagram, hoping to glean whatever I could to help me score more goals. As my game was based around using my pace to get in behind defences, he seemed the perfect role model. And the movement off the ball that was his strength was to become my key asset.

I was also keen to listen to, and learn from, the excellent teachers I was encountering at Cambridge. Although I'd managed to impress enough to be retained on the books for three straight years, I remained very aware of both the limitations of my game – I still recognised a technical deficit from those missing early years – and the likelihood of somebody better being found by the club. A reasonable assumption seeing as almost all the boys I had, at one point or another, lined up alongside at the centre of excellence were now no longer there. So I needed to keep learning, keep improving.

Soon after my 12th birthday, I was granted an even greater learning opportunity. A letter came through the door at home. It was printed, tantalisingly, on FA-headed paper. I was invited to Oakham School for a get-together of boys in the Midlands area recommended by their clubs for FA monitoring. To say I was excited would be something of an understatement.

There were boys from Ipswich (including Kieron Dyer), Luton (including Matt Upson), Aston Villa, Stoke (including John Curtis), Port Vale, Coventry (including John Eustace) and many more. The well-respected John Peacock (later to manage

England under-17s to two world titles) was the chief coach. The sessions were intricate and skills-based, and the step up in level was very evident. But I held my own, and loved the extra quality of through-ball on offer that meant fewer of my runs went unrewarded.

Mum and Dad were soon sent a report detailing how I'd done (pretty well as it turned out), along with an invitation to a follow-up in April. I went back to training at Cambridge and matches at Mildenhall with an extra spring in my step. But by the time the next meeting with the FA development squad came around, that spring had all but disappeared.

3

The Great Escape

Dad was diagnosed with pancreatic cancer around Christmas, and pretty soon it was clear that no treatment was going to be able to save him. Mum cared for him at home for his final few months and it was difficult seeing him deteriorate, although occasionally you could catch a boyish grin as he dreamt about seeing a goal go in and let out a faint cheer – whether those goals were being scored by Jimmy Greaves, his boyhood idol, or by me, I'll never know. But it was nice to see him capable of being happy right until the end.

The end actually came while I was away at Leicester University with the FA. I can still remember the coaches seeming to go a bit overboard on the praise when I scored a good goal, and also when I answered the tie-break question of the quiz (well, they didn't call me Statto for nothing) on the final day. Both those incidents came after Mum had let them know what had finally and inevitably happened on the Wednesday night.

When I got home, the news about Dad – as he was a well-known and popular man in Mildenhall – was the headline story plastered over the front page of the local paper. That prompted a few tears, but only a few. I think people thought I was bottling stuff up, but I wasn't in denial, I just felt more comfortable in stoic mode. I was genuinely more worried about the effect on Mum and my brother.

Andrew, being only ten, had found the whole episode hard to compute. I remember thinking back to the Hillsborough disaster (Dad died on its third anniversary), which had made me bawl my eyes out at the thought of so many children never getting to see their dads again (my nine-year-old imagination had assumed that all those who died were men with children).

In my head, my brother was now like one of them. Mum, on top of the emotional turmoil she must have been going through over the past few months, now had to find the time, energy and logistical nous to ferry two football-mad boys all over the place to their various commitments.

I wanted to be strong for both of them.

Football was such an amazing escape from it all for me. When I arrived home from Leicester, I was almost straight off on another football break, this time with the Ashworths in Great Yarmouth, as the slow merger between Paul's PASS soccer school and the Cambridge youth system started to gather pace. We'd already been to the Ayr Cup, an excellent youth tournament – where Paul informed me that a Celtic scout had enquired about me – and that summer we headed off to Västerås, Sweden for the Aros Cup, an international competition spanning many age groups. Having the football to focus on was such a relief as it offered precious little time to think about events at home. I remember trying unsuccessfully to stifle some crying one night in Sweden, when it was so hot I struggled to sleep and I couldn't help my mind wandering. But mostly I was able to pour myself completely into the tournament atmosphere and concentrate on my performances. It certainly worked as Paul and Danny awarded me their player of the tournament accolade. I even scored my penalty as, being stereotypically English, we exited in the quarter-finals via a shoot-out.

Coming home from Sweden and not being able to tell Dad all about it was probably when I felt saddest of all. I so missed talking with him about the game; it was one of the hardest things to get over. But, over time, I was able to come to terms with it. Mum was a very able deputy, always interested and wanting to chat. And the best way to keep my spirits up was to keep playing. As the new season started, the football came thick and fast.

Mildenhall matches on Sundays and training one evening a week. Cambridge training on Monday evenings. School games during the week or sometimes on Saturdays. Half-terms away with PASS. FA development meet-ups periodically.

Cambs Colts League (where Mildenhall had switched from the Thetford League) representative side matches every so often. But, looking back, while of course I loved the matches, it was only the training that was really doing anything to improve my prospects as a player.

The matches offered a competitive environment in which to test yourself, so had value in learning to apply skills under some form of pressure, but the skill-set encouraged was so narrow due to the size of the pitches involved. As players it was easy to become pigeon-holed from a young age, just honing the skills that helped you succeed in whatever role you filled; the things that would make you stand out and be noticed. As I was quick and wanted to be Gary Lineker, I played up front. But probably 80 per cent of my goals came in exactly the same fashion – a through ball either slid through or clipped over the defence for me to run on to, and either round the goalkeeper if he came out, or slot it past him into the vast expanse of goal either side if he didn't. While there was nothing wrong with practising those particular skills over and over again, as scoring goals will always attract attention, it was never going to make for a particularly well-rounded player.

So the training and coaching I was receiving, with Gary, with Paul and with Spider, was so vital. In training, you worked in tight areas, such as small squares, so close control was imperative. In 11 vs 11 matches, there was so much space your first touch was rarely taken under great pressure. In training we did passing drills to work on our accuracy. In matches I didn't have much cause to pass the ball save for the odd short lay-off to a team-mate so I could make another forward run.

Even with coaching, though, some areas slipped through the net. At one of the FA get-togethers, we did a long passing drill. I paired up with Matt Upson – we'd previously played in the same Thetford & District League representative side as his local side was Scole. Matt was a big lad and his sweet left foot could effortlessly caress the ball aerially over 30 yards or so. I was tiny (Tiny Tom no less) and had neither the power nor the technique to reciprocate. But then I think that was probably the first time I had ever tried. I hardly had to pass the ball at all in most matches, even on the ground, and particularly not over a greater distance than ten yards or so.

Aside from the pitch size issue, maybe if everyone was encouraged to play in all positions as a youngster, and be less defined by role until later in their development, it would improve things. This is the kind of all-round development they speak of at places like Barcelona and Ajax. Certainly if I'd had to play in midfield or at full-back sometimes while growing up, I would have learned better how to pick out and deliver the same passes that I revelled in receiving as a forward. As my career progressed, as I will discuss later, I would certainly live to regret not having worked on a wider range of skills in match conditions in my youth.

But that just wasn't how things were done. Like the parents who couldn't help but holler ridiculously unhelpful 'advice' from the touchline, so many of the men in charge of the youth teams I played against thought of their teams as mini versions of the professional teams they followed on a Saturday. Whose only purpose is to win. Not development. Not enjoyment (primarily). Winning.

Thankfully, Spider wasn't really one of them – we always rotated our players, for example, so everyone had to take their turn on the bench – although even he crossed the line on occasion, particularly as we got a bit older. While anyone who gives up their time to organise a youth team and provide an outlet for young people should be lauded, too many of them seemed to be frustrated senior team managers, with which came an in-built need to win, to prove themselves worthy of the job. I've lost count of the amount of times I attended an end-of-season youth league awards ceremony and saw a 'manager' holding the trophy aloft, as if he was the reason the league or cup had been won. They are the types that have forced the FA to impose a blanket ban on the publishing of scores and League tables in early youth football. To stop the cult of youth 'managers' eschewing development to feed their own egos.

The key point, though, whether local papers carry the scores or not, is that the kids themselves want to win anyway. I always wanted to win. So did my mates. We put ourselves under that pressure, and were gutted when we lost. All youngsters are. But they also want to play freely and express themselves. Any outside pressure for victory – be it in the form of team selection or imposed tactics – can only suppress that.

After a couple more regional get-togethers, in 1993 came my big invitation from the FA: the first round of trials for the FA National School at Lilleshall. The long drive to Shropshire (further elongated by the fact I left my tie at home, only realising near Cambridge!) was made worthwhile as I performed well in the 11-a-side matches, which were interspersed with fitness testing and small training sessions for those awaiting their next turn under the microscope. Having scored a well-taken goal and turned defenders on a number of occasions, I felt reasonably confident as a proud Mum took me home.

Sure enough, the next letter said I had advanced to the final trial, with about 40 boys from all over the country competing for those 16 hallowed spots on the roll-call, following in the footsteps of Sol Campbell, Andy Cole, Nicky Barmby and others. Within minutes it was such an obvious step-up in quality, both from the trial before and from the Cambs Colts League games which still accounted for most of my time on the pitch. Other than John Curtis, I didn't recognise too many of the other boys, although I now know them to have included Michael Branch (of Everton), Mark Gower (of Spurs) and Jody Morris and Neil Clement (of Chelsea). I partnered Branch in the first game, with little success, as we both constantly wanted to stretch the back four, with neither of us coming towards the ball to help build play. On the few occasions our runs were picked out, though, he certainly looked the part more than I did. He was quicker, bigger, stronger and looked technically better as well. I knew I would have to up my game in the further rounds of matches.

I tried my best, but couldn't make it happen. The giant Matthew Wicks (son of Chelsea legend Steve) proved too formidable a centre-half in one game, and then a lad from Leeds – whose diminutive stature, similar to mine, gave me hope that I could be more competitive – seemed to read my every intention in the last outing. He marked me out of the game, and out of contention. Although I did manage to latch onto one nice through ball (from Wicks, ironically enough) and slot home neatly, I knew it hadn't been enough. When John Peacock wished me well in saying goodbye, there was a resigned air of finality about it.

And so I was left to watch on TV a year or so later as the England schoolboy team, captained by Curtis and spearheaded by Branch, became record-breakers by winning all of their season's fixtures. I could comfort myself in recognising how far I'd got in appearing in that trial, along with some relief at not having had to leave home at 14 to live on the other side of the country. I wasn't ready for that, and as a footballer I clearly wasn't yet ready to keep such illustrious company, either on a physical or technical level.

But the FA was soon to ensure that, from that point on, I would be keeping a much higher standard of footballing company every week. The foibles and flaws of Sunday League youth football were no longer a concern once the 1993/94 season kicked into gear, as professional teams were given a structure in which they could face each other. Like a regionalised mini Football League, only with no-one keeping score or tables. It was really exciting to be able to pull on an actual Cambridge United shirt each Sunday (even if it was a well-used, slightly out-of-date version of the first team's), and that was certainly when the realisation of professionalism, and what it meant, started to bed in.

The team talks, with Paul in charge of my under-14 group, were suddenly more cutting and critical at times, but also much more insightful. Playing against better players and teams every week – well, most weeks; we beat Northampton 10-0 so Paul sent the under-13s to the corresponding away fixture! – with an astute coach to act as a guide, the potential for development was hugely increased compared to the provincial stuff we'd all been playing. Much as I had enjoyed every minute of my Mildenhall Town youth days, this was a welcome step up.

In just our second game, I scored a hat-trick as we beat Ipswich 4-0 on the training pitch sited next to their Portman Road home. And on September 14th 1993, I signed schoolboy forms on the Abbey pitch at half-time of the first team's 2-0 win over Swansea. I celebrated that with braces in impressive wins at the plush training grounds of Leicester and Derby, and would go on to net 38 times in 31 games that season. I actually managed to score at least once against every different team we faced. I know this detail because, true to my nature, I kept stats of the whole season, including the player ratings for each game that Paul would send to us via letter. As the first team, following John Beck's sacking, were finally suffering from vertigo and had begun to tumble down the divisions to their more natural home in the fourth tier, we were proving very competitive with renowned opponents such as the afore-mentioned as well as Norwich and Nottingham Forest.

At the end of an impressive season, we enjoyed another sojourn on the continent, this time at the Dana Cup in Hjørring, Denmark. It was another superb international tournament which gave us valuable experience of facing players from all over the world – even as far afield as South America – with their different styles and speeds of play. We continued our good form from the previous nine months to reach the final, eventually losing to a far superior Swiss side.

I signed off the summer with another call-up from the FA for a training camp, this time for the purpose of a warm-up game for the national side that I (and all the boys present) had been overlooked for a year earlier. Just five minutes in, I got on the end of a clever reverse pass and buried a left-footed shot into the far corner. How good that felt.

But with England asserting their class as the game went on to run out 3-1 winners, the post-match address from John Peacock contained a hint to the challenges I would soon be facing. He'd brought me off early in the second half, and said at the end that he'd needed to get a bit of pace into our forward line to help us get a foothold in the game. Pace had always been my thing, but that seemed to have changed over the previous few months.

I'd always been reasonably small, but over the summer it seemed like I didn't change a bit, while everyone else started the journey towards manhood. In the team photo from our under-15 season, I look like the mascot. But unlike the FA trials, where age groups were based on school years and with an August 31st birthday I was as young as it was possible to be, here I was actually the oldest player (football competition age groups running from August 1st to July 31st). I was just a (very) late developer.

This brought with it some difficulties. Paul had passed on our side into the charge of Michael Cook, a member of the first-team squad at Wembley four years earlier whose career was cut short by a knee injury. After the first five games, in which I was largely anonymous and barely had a shot let alone scored a goal, Cooky singled me out in the team talk ahead of a home match with Mansfield.

"I've been told a lot about you," he said. "About how you're this and you're that. Well, we've had five games now and I've not seen anything. You can't just hang around up front hoping everyone else will do the work for you. If you're going to be a striker for me, you'd better start getting hold of the ball for us and bringing other players into play. If I don't see any of that in the first 25 minutes (the matches were split into three 25-minute sections), you're coming off."

I was a bit shocked at his directness, but he was right. Over the past year under Paul's tutelage, I had learnt the importance of a striker being an able target man, reliable at retaining possession to help the team make their way up the field. But I still wouldn't have called it a strength of mine, playing with my back to goal. It was more a necessary evil that had to be endured to create more opportunities for yourself. My first touch was decent, but it was a very different skill trying to bring the ball under control while simultaneously having to physically resist a big defender coming at you from behind. Which is why I much preferred running them the other way, especially when I knew that nine times out of ten I would win the race. But not anymore. It felt more like two or three times out of ten, if I was lucky. So I had to embrace showing to receive the ball. And thanks to Cooky's ultimatum, I had to do it well in the next 25 minutes.

Mercifully, I did. I kept offering myself and managed to get hold of the ball on the majority of occasions. We scored three times directly from my involvements, even though I didn't score any of them. "That's more like it," said Cooky at the break. And so from that coach's challenge, the rest of my career developed, really.

I knew that, until I caught up physically, if I ever did, I couldn't be Gary Lineker. And as he'd retired, I had the perfect new hero in the Tottenham forward line. So I started to study Teddy Sheringham. His biggest strength, other than being a superb finisher, was in always being available, picking up positions where defenders were uncomfortable going and thereby creating space either for himself or colleagues. Those became key aims of mine.

I still wanted to score goals. Of course. I still wanted to get in behind defences whenever possible. But I had to recognise that it wouldn't be quite so easy, at least for a while, and if I was to remain a functioning member of the team, and stay on course for my dream of becoming a professional, I had to rely more on speed of thought than fleet of foot. Which could only be better for my all-round game in the long term, even if I did grow and regain my pace. And as I never really did, it was an even more vital development for me.

Towards the end of the campaign, we went to a training camp with Peterborough, at Fairthorn Manor, near Southampton. The extremely intimidating Boro coach Bob Higgins led the week. Aside from football, we had to partake in team building exercises, like assault courses and abseiling. All straightforward enough, until it came to 'The Den'. This was where Cambridge and Peterborough – including future Premier League star Simon 'Digger' Davies – were lined up ten yards from each other, and one by one called in for a 'fight' with an opposing team member. Punches were banned but slapping allowed, though the distinction between the two was blurred as a couple of lads were poleaxed. Luckily, I managed to ensure my match-up descended pretty quickly into wrestling, and it was called a draw. Whether it was designed to toughen us up, I'm not entirely sure. It all seemed a bit sadistic to me.

But football-wise, the week went very well. We swapped managers for a day and, after our win over Portsmouth, Bob told me that "any team needs a forward who can keep hold of the ball as well as you". I was delighted with that. Along with plenty of kind words I'd had from Cooky, it further helped to restore my confidence, which had been badly dented in the early months of the season when all the main tenets of my game were crumbling around me. The re-invention seemed worthwhile.

4

His Name is Rio

As soon as the 1994/95 season was finished (including another trip to the Dana Cup, where we were knocked out by bitter rivals Peterborough and from where I returned home – much to Mum's disgust – with a shaved head), football had to take a back seat for a few months. My GCSEs took centre stage.

The rest of my Cambridge team (who were not due to do their exams for another year) went back down to Southampton for a few days with Bob. I received the invite, but phoned to let him know that I couldn't make it. There were some minor insinuations that it might show I wasn't fully committed to football (one team-mate was in the same August birthday boat as me, and decided to go), but I knew what was more important to me. My education.

I desperately wanted to be a professional footballer. I couldn't think of a better job to do in the world. But I wasn't going to reduce my other options by sacrificing my studies for a training camp. A training camp that would be long forgotten by the time the new season rolled around. I'd seen about a hundred boys let go by Cambridge – just in my age group – in the six years I'd been on the books. I wasn't arrogant or stupid enough to believe that graduating to the professional ranks was a sure thing. So I was always just as focused on school.

Obviously it helped that I was a bright lad who'd always excelled in class, and who had a desire, because of that, to get the best results possible. For those not so academically inclined, it was so easy for football to dominate their lives to the exclusion of everything else. And those subtle hints from coaches, that anything other than complete concentration on football weakened your prospects within the game, only fed into that dangerous mind-set.

Twenty years on, in the era of £300,000-a-week Premier League contracts, the temptation to put all your eggs into football's basket must be so great. But many who, at 14 or 15 – when the GCSE cycle is in full flow – look like world-beaters and certain superstars, are merely early bloomers whose talents are amplified by their physical superiority. When this wanes over the next few years, as others catch up, they are downgraded from 'certain superstar' to 'decent player'. And that seemingly guaranteed jackpot, which meant they would never have to work for a living, is also downgraded. 'Decent players' can still earn a good wage from the game, but there are a few more of them around and the competition is fierce. So they may not. And either way, they're going to need another job at some point. I never saw accepting that possibility as a lack of confidence or ambition, or some kind of admission that I was not up to scratch, as many my age might have regarded such a viewpoint at the time. I just saw it as realistic. So while I was going to give my absolute all in pursuit of my footballing dreams, I was going to do likewise with my schoolwork.

After spending a great summer celebrating my exam results, pre-season began with a few of us from the now under-16s invited to train with the youth team, under new manager Peter Brabrook, the former West Ham winger. Previous boss Tommy Taylor – who had seemed to take a bit of a shine to me on the latest Denmark trip, where the youth team joined us – had moved up to take charge of the first team, newly relegated to Division Three.

From those few training sessions, it was clear that this youth team was not a vintage crop. Tommy's team the year before were a powerful and skilful outfit who could hold their own against the powerhouses of the South East Counties League: Arsenal, Chelsea, Tottenham, West Ham et al. The new intake (albeit with a slightly weakened team) struggled to cope with a pre-season friendly at local side Haverhill Rovers. I was given an hour in a 2-1 defeat which had Pete steaming from the ears, a fact not helped by his post-match dressing down being interrupted by the theme tune of a hand-held console game blasting out from one of the lads' pockets. I was neat and tidy enough in the game, just as I had been in training, which no doubt prompted Pete to give me a game. But I didn't really make much of an impact, so I was somewhat surprised when I was called up to the bench for the first League game of the season, at home to Spurs, a couple of weeks later.

I didn't get on, thankfully. We were given a footballing lesson by a team including Stephen (son of Ray) Clemence in midfield and Rory Allen up front. 7-0. Results didn't improve as the weeks wore on. 6-1 to Arsenal. 7-1 to Chelsea. 3-0 at Shrewsbury in the FA Youth Cup, the day only notable for me – as eventually I didn't even make the bench – due to being approached by police, while I waited in a lay-by for my lift, on suspicion of being a rent boy.

Pete left and returned, I believe, to a well-respected role in the West Ham academy. He was replaced by David Batch, a former right back in the Cambridge youth team who, at 23, became the youngest incumbent of such a role at a professional club in England. Batchy was a friend of the Ashworths and I'd had a few sessions with him at various times in the younger age groups, so knew him fairly well. I sensed his appointment might grant me some early opportunities to establish myself at youth team level, particularly given the team's current struggles. I was right.

Within a couple of weeks I'd made an impression as a substitute against QPR, and a week later came my full youth team debut. We were at home to West Ham, and all the talk among the lads was about their centre-half. I'd never heard of Rio Ferdinand. "Is he anything to do with Les?" I asked. "Cousins," came the response. "But he's on a different planet, Rio. Banker to captain England one day, they reckon." Not at all daunting for me, then, as a short, skinny 16 year old about to play two years above his age group for the first time.

Everything went pretty well, though. I got hold of the ball when I needed to, linked play capably and, though Mr Ferdinand didn't see fit to give me a sniff of goal, my strike partner Trevor Benjamin (who could cause even the most celebrated of defenders problems with his sheer physicality) forced his way through to equalise with ten minutes left. The only thing to spoil the day was the Hammers grabbing a winner deep into stoppage time. They'd also opened the scoring deep into stoppage time at the end of the first half. Both goals were a bit scrappy, a loose ball bouncing around the box before being dispatched crisply into the net. Funnily enough, the scorer of both hadn't been given quite as glowing a reference as Rio from the lads before the game. "Fat bastard," they said. "Thinks he's made it big already. Barely got a kick last time." Probably scored, though. And Frank Lampard certainly proved the match-winner here.

I'd done enough to keep my place and next we came up against Arsenal, again at home. Bottom against top. But competing well with West Ham had bred a certain belief in our team, and we raced into a 2-0 lead. Despite being pegged back to 2-2 by half-time, we came out unbowed after the interval. My moment arrived around the hour mark. Trev arrowed a cross in from the left wing and I got across the face of the centre-half and volleyed home. My first ever youth team goal. And against Arsenal. I was dancing on air for the rest of the game, and went on to supply the pass for Trev's clinching goal late on.

I also picked up my first ever yellow card. As would become a feature for me throughout my career, Batchy had entrusted me with concentrating enough when the ball went dead to make sure Arsenal were not allowed to take any quick set-pieces. I was perhaps a bit too obvious with my delaying tactic on one occasion, and the referee took umbrage. At least – as Cambridge were not yet actually employing me – the ensuing fine couldn't be docked from my wages and the club footed the bill.

From that day, buoyed by my goal, I started to feel more comfortable at youth team level. I adjusted to both the huge increase in speed of play from the under-16s, and the fact that I was effectively now playing against men who could swat me aside like an irritant fly if I didn't hold my ground strongly enough. Goals against Charlton and a brace against Leyton Orient followed as our points tally slowly grew.

Our best win came at Spurs, revenge for that opening day mauling. From 2-0 down we stormed back to win 3-2, and I'll never forget the lack of grace in defeat from the shell-shocked Premier League youngsters. Half of them wouldn't even shake our hands, traipsing straight off to receive a bollocking. Some people will tell you that there's nothing wrong with that, that good losers are just losers, blah blah blah. But sometimes a bit of humility can't hurt; the mere act of having to congratulate your conquerors – particularly if they are 'below' you in the football food chain – can help to drive you in not wanting to feel that way again. Instead, they just came across as the football equivalent of spoilt little rich kids being upstaged by urchins they deemed unworthy of sharing a pitch with them.

The day was bittersweet for me, though. I remember experiencing the jubilation in the dressing room afterwards with a sense of distance. I hadn't played well. Sure, I'd worked hard. 'Put in a shift' as they say in football. Done my bit to delay any possible quick free-kicks from Spurs to allow everyone time to regain shape and switch on. But all that was a given, for me. I'd never expect any undue praise simply for working hard and applying myself mentally. Those were strengths of mine – fitness, concentration, game intelligence – which I was glad to possess and helped to give me an edge over some other players. But they were only foundations – I was a footballer and if I didn't deliver on the ball, it wasn't good enough. Particularly as I was playing against much older players who could physically dominate me, I had to make sure the technical side of my game was spot on.

And on that day it wasn't. I could always live with not looking like scoring if I'd contributed well to the team's attacking play, but here I'd lost the ball too easily on a few occasions, and many of my attempts to play a clever or creative pass had gone awry. It was reflective of a dip in form I'd noticed gather slow momentum for a while. Perhaps I was a bit drained, physically and mentally from acclimatising to the higher level over the past few months. Batchy noticed me looking a bit down and tried to reassure me about my performance, but after another poor showing a week later, against a Carl Cort-inspired Wimbledon,

I was taken out of the firing line for a couple of weeks.

So I was on the bench for our critical final game of the season, at home to Chelsea. Lose and we would finish bottom of the league, with a possible demotion to the South East Counties League Division Two in the offing. Which would mean missing out on testing ourselves against the big boys with whom we'd learnt to compete since Batchy's arrival. A draw might be enough to see off Fulham and stay up. Shortly after half-time, we were 2-0 down and looking beaten. I was sent on to freshen things up, and immediately felt brighter than in my previous few outings. Within minutes I had won a penalty to get us back in it, and this proved the catalyst to a siege on the Chelsea goal. Eventually, with the referee poised to blow for full-time, our goalkeeper Shaun Marshall launched a huge kick upfield and his none-more-Norfolk dad bellowed "get on yer bike, Tom!" I threw myself at the ball as it dropped right on the edge of the Chelsea box, hoping to connect with a volley before the ball bounced and became an easy claim for the goalkeeper. The ball landed square on my knee, but it did the trick and flew into the corner for a last-gasp equaliser.

It being a nice, warm spring day, quite a crowd had turned up for the match – by youth team standards – and so a pretty big cheer went up when my goal went in. Coupled with the feeling of importance due to our relegation plight, it was my first real experience of the extra frisson that crowd noise could add to the already very satisfying feeling of scoring a goal. I wanted more.

For some of my under-16 team-mates, though, there would be no 'more'. A few weeks earlier had come decision time on the boys in my age group. To be an apprentice, or not to be. For the few who had already been settling in at youth team level, there was no tension. The decision had already been made. The week in Southampton was just a coronation of their soon-to-be YTS status. For me, it was just a training camp. Being a school year older than my team-mates, I was already halfway through my A-levels, with Cambridge seeming perfectly happy that I would continue to play at weekends while not training during the week.

For the rest of the boys, the whole situation felt apocalyptic. They'd all devoted themselves to training, games and tournaments abroad over the last few years, with the goal of becoming an apprentice. Finally being paid (even if it was only a pittance) to play football. And moving closer to the ultimate dream of being a professional. But after a few brutal minutes in a room with Paul, for some it was all over. There was heartbreak. There was a lot of shouting, much of it espousing a defiant, 'I'll show them' attitude that masked huge disappointment. In the era now of X Factor and a million other reality TV shows, it's the kind of 'boot camp' scenario that everyone is familiar with.

Those released really should have seen it coming. As an exercise, seeing as I wasn't having to have the same discussion as everyone else, Paul asked me in for a chat and wondered if I could predict the fates of my team-mates. I called them all correctly. So if I could work it out, I'm sure they all could, if they considered it honestly. But clearly it came as a big shock to one or two. And it was painful to watch them suffer that blow. All you could do was offer condolence and tell them they might get a chance with another club if they kept working at it. Some even do. But none of them did.

Hopefully, though, as dispiriting and upsetting as the rejection was, they would ultimately come to recognise the good part football had played in their lives, and the skills – not on the pitch, but off – it had given them. To have survived in the youth set-up at a professional club for any length of time, they had to have shown dedication and a healthy work ethic. They had to have learnt to deal with and respond to criticism. They had to have been able to follow instructions, to function well within a team unit, but at the same time excel as an individual and know that sometimes you can back your own instincts to do something less prescribed for everyone's benefit (even if you do get an earful, on occasion, when it goes horribly wrong!). And they had to have developed at least some strength of character to recover from setbacks: poor performances, missed chances, mistakes leading to goals conceded and so on. This was just a slightly bigger setback to deal with. But all of those skills are foundations for success in any field. Things that employers look for. Though of course I'm sure none of them were thinking this at the time.

The next season soon came around – for those who made the cut – but it started badly for me. In a pre-season friendly I broke a bone for the first and, as yet, only time. A big centre-half from Barnet fell on me, his knee snapping my collar bone. I missed the next six weeks while I healed, including the first five games of the season. Happily, Batchy was glad to get me back in the team as soon as possible, and I scored the goals that got us through to the FA Youth Cup first round, where we were to face Colchester at home.

Our FA Youth Cup games were always played under lights at the Abbey Stadium in front of paying supporters, which added a real sense of occasion. And for me, it turned out to be quite an occasion. A life-changing one.

The tie fell during the first week of Roy McFarland's tenure as Cambridge United manager, Tommy Taylor having left for Leyton Orient. And the former England captain came along to see what was on offer in the youth team. After a scrappy first half in which we took an early lead but came in deservedly 2-1 down, Roy pretty much took over the half-time team talk – not that I think Batchy was too pleased – and, after a few general comments, re-organised the team. "The little lad needs to be in behind the front two," he said, referring to me. That was how we often played anyway, I'd just been shifted out to the left for this particular match.

After the restart we duly conceded twice in the opening five minutes to kill off the game. But we went on to play some really good stuff, and I was at the heart of most of it, even grabbing a consolation goal at the end of a flowing team move. We made our way into the dressing room, where Roy was ready for us. But far from starting a dissection of the game, his first words were "What's your name, son?" He was looking at me. I answered him. "You can play," he continued. "This one can play," he told the rest of the boys. It felt like for the next five minutes he was just describing to everyone what he'd liked about my performance and what I'd done well. It was a bit surreal, but obviously welcome from my point of view. "You're still at school, yes?" he asked, which was probably a natural presumption given my size. I somewhat disingenuously agreed; though it was technically true, it implied that I was younger than the other lads even though I was older than half of them. But it didn't hurt to further the idea of my precociousness in my new admirer. I laughed in nervous embarrassment discussing the whole episode with the lads once Roy had left. But inside I felt on top of the world.

Over the next few months, Roy came to a few of our games on Saturday mornings, when the first team were also at home. I managed to build on my good first impression with some decent performances. But the issue of what to do with me at the end of the season, when I completed sixth form, was yet to be sorted. The discrepancy between my school and footballing age groups had certainly worked to my advantage. I'd wanted to do my A-levels and, because of the date of my birthday, I'd done so without appearing to choose them over a YTS place. But the club were unsure whether they could offer me a one-year apprenticeship, to take me up to the point when decisions on professional contracts were made (the standard scheme places ran for two years). So the matter was still up in the air. Then a letter came through my – and the club's – door which settled everything.

It was the FA getting in touch again, after a two-year hiatus. The England Schools under-18 team needed a warm-up game ahead of a European tournament they were headed to. So a lot of the boys from those Midlands development squads (future Watford captain John Eustace was a fellow call-up) were summoned to Lowestoft Town's Crown Meadow.

There was suddenly a bit of a panic at Cambridge. By playing in this game I could possibly be putting myself in the shop window, while all that actually attached me to the club in any formal way – despite being at United since the age of ten – were League and cup registration forms. So Batchy phoned Mum to ask if we would like to come in to the club offices to discuss a professional contract. Having played the second half of the FA game up front, and performed pretty well according the coach in charge, I spent the next afternoon in the rickety old Portakabin club offices at the Abbey, with Roy, a proud Mum and a just as proud Batchy.

As my A Level exams were fast approaching, I'd just heard back from Birmingham University regarding my application to study law there. Providing I met my predicted grades of an A and two Bs, I'd secured a place there for the next three years. Great news. But for me it was strictly a fall-back option. Once I'd been in to see Roy, there was only one deal I was interested in.

I was offered a two-year contract, starting at £85 a week and rising to £115 in the second year. I was so excited I would have agreed to anything, so after a half-hour chat, we shook hands. A few days later, the formal offer came through the post, signed by Steve Greenall, the club secretary. Somewhat bizarrely, the papers in front of me now indicated a three-year contract, starting at £135 a week, then rising to £175 and £200 in the final year. I didn't know whether to say something or just sign all the copies and send them back before anyone could notice the mistake!

The moral dilemma didn't last long as the next day brought a phone call from a rather sheepish Steve. He apologised, explained there had been some crossed wires between him and Roy, and informed me that he would have to reduce the length of the contract offered to the expected two years. "I can't renege on the money though," he added. "So the two years will be on the terms as presented in the first two years of that contract."

But I couldn't really care less about the money. All I cared about was that I was guaranteed a chance to train with the first team and prove myself able to play at that level. I still fully expected to be in the youth team with my long-standing teammates for most of the next season, but I knew that at some point over the next two years I would get an opportunity to mix with the senior players. And with a bit of luck and hard work, maybe even get a shot at the Football League.

5

Watch Out, Beadle's About

My first foray into Football League action was to come somewhat sooner than expected. As I reported back for my opening days as a bona fide professional footballer, I was still very much a member of the youth team. While Batchy wouldn't let me clean any boots ("You'll need a boot boy yourself, soon enough" was his logic), I played my part in the morning jobs: getting all the first-team training equipment ready, making sure all the balls were pumped up and so on. But after an impressive first four matches of the season, including goals against Norwich and Arsenal, one Friday – two days before my 18th birthday – I was invited to train with the first team.

At the end of the session, as we convened back at the Abbey, the squad of 15 was pinned up for the following day's visit of Shrewsbury. And I was in it. The *Cambridge Evening News* was full of local-boy-done-good cheer at my inclusion, but I didn't end up making the substitutes' bench. Picked up a nice tip about not wearing a club tie to games, though. "Makes you look like the chairman's grandson," advised Ian Ashbee. And I didn't have to wait long for a brief taste of the limelight.

On the Monday I was named as sub for the reserves at Colchester – the first time I'd ever been involved in the ressies. My old under-15 boss Cooky was in charge, which helped me feel at home. In true Roy of the Rovers fashion, I was brought on with 15 minutes left and, with my first touch, burst through onto a knockdown from Trevor Benjamin before steadying myself to drive into the far corner. That my second involvement in the game was a horribly miscued clearance, which nearly put the home side in on goal, didn't seem to matter too much when the ref called time on our 3-2 victory, making me the match-winner.

The next day saw Colchester's first team come to the Abbey, and my dream debut for the reserves earned me a spot on the bench this time. Once braces from Martin Butler and John Taylor had given us the comfort of a 4-1 lead, I was granted a few minutes on the pitch. A few seconds in, Ben Chenery got in behind on the right and slid the ball back to me about 15 yards out. A repeat of the day before looked on the cards as I made a good connection towards the far corner, only for a desperate block to deny me.

On the Thursday, I was asked to find a spot in the first-team dressing room and train with them every day. On the Friday – though I wasn't included on the trip – the first team won 2-0 at Tommy Taylor's Leyton Orient to go top of the league. A perfect end to a pretty perfect week. That perfection couldn't last, however.

It was 15 games before Cambridge United tasted victory again. And my euphoric breakthrough to first-team contention gave way to a more problematic spell. Having starred and scored for the reserves at Peterborough (where Paul Ashworth, who'd moved on to the Posh, described me as the best player on the pitch), I was drafted back into the youth team for a big FA Youth Cup game. I played poorly as we were knocked out, in embarrassing fashion, at home to local non-League side Somersham, whose sickening cheers echoed around a largely empty Abbey Stadium. In many cases this would have been seen as a player getting too big for his boots after promotion to the senior side. There was no question of that. If anything, for me it was precisely the opposite.

I was yet to feel fully at home and comfortable that I belonged in the first-team set-up. This was the first time in my life that I'd trained every day, and after only a few weeks with the youth team – where mistakes were more frequent and standards more forgiving – I'd been catapulted up to play with experienced pros; players used to performing well, day in, day out for years. People like David Preece, our assistant manager and former Luton legend, John Taylor (better known as 'Shaggy'), Cambridge's all-time leading scorer and Colin Foster ('Fozzie'), the ex-Nottingham Forest centre-half.

I was doubting myself on a daily basis. Though I'd seen enough to know that at my best I could certainly compete, and not look out of place, I also felt a lot of pressure to deliver a wider set of skills more consistently. Drills where a variety of ranges of passing were required had the capacity to make you look stupid if you couldn't match the quality of the rest of the group, many of whom made it look effortless. There were still a few slices and shanks – after all, it was Cambridge United, not Manchester United – but for me it was sometimes a bit like that long-passing session opposite Matt Upson at the FA course, six years previously. Only this time if you got it wrong, it was in full view of the manager you were supposed to be trying to impress, not merely an FA coach whom you might never see again.

I also developed a love/hate relationship with Friday training sessions. Love because it was five-a-side, which was certainly one of my strengths and therefore a favourite of mine. Hate because it was only enjoyable if my team went in front early or looked to be in the ascendancy in the opening stages. Otherwise, the dreaded 'Yellow Jersey' would start to loom large. The 'yellow' was given to the player deemed the worst performer in the five-a-side, to be worn the following week. It was never washed and had phrases like 'I've had a stinker' and 'I'm shite' daubed on it in felt tip.

If you made a mistake in the game, the lads would start chanting 'yeeellllooooow' at you. I would come to appreciate it as good fun as I got older and more established, and it was probably a gentle introduction to the real pressure of starting a first-team game poorly but needing the conviction to keep playing and taking chances, even when any further mistakes could prove costly. But in those early months I couldn't bear the thought of being 'awarded' the 'yellow'. The young players were always the most vulnerable to being targeted, and, a bit like messing up in the passing drills, I equated 'yellow' status with appearing sub-standard in the gaffer's eyes. I'm sure that was never really the case, that he could see past it and make up his own mind, but that's not how it felt at the time.

The desire for the gaffer to associate only positive thoughts with me also led, bizarrely, to an act so out of character, I can still barely believe it happened. Midway through the team's winless run came a particularly disheartening 1-0 home defeat to lowly Hull. Supporter patience was wearing thin and the reaction at the end of the game was pretty foreboding. I wasn't involved on the night, and wanted to make a quick getaway to rest and prepare for the reserve game the next day, sensing that the gaffer may be forced into changes. Struggling to get out of a ridiculously tight parking space that a steward had squeezed me into, I thought I'd wriggled clear only to feel my back end clip the car beside me.

Realising straight away that the vehicle in question was the company car of Ken, our physio, I knew that to fess up immediately would mean having to go into the changing room where the gaffer was probably turning the air blue. Not wanting Roy to link, in any way, that turgid performance with me, I panicked and drove off. If that doesn't sound a particularly rational explanation, it's because it isn't one. Apparently I even almost hit our captain Paul Wanless's youngest daughter on the way out of the ground, which put me firmly out of his good books for a few weeks. Certainly not my proudest moment. I came clean to Ken the next morning and paid the club's £18 bill for a new number plate. At training, the lads (apart from Wanny, obviously) found it hilarious. I was just cringing.

There was only one way I could see to start feeling more capable and confident in first-team training. Only one way to be more concerned with making the gaffer notice me for positive reasons, rather than fretting about him seeing my mistakes: extra practice. Roy had obviously seen enough from me to elevate me into the first-team picture, but it was a big step up and I had a lot of catching up to do. Even our younger players (and by budgetary necessity we were a youthful squad) seemed like veterans compared to me. Factor in their youth team days and most of them had four or more years of training every day under their belts. I had three months.

Doing extra at the training ground was not always an option, as players shared lifts on the painstakingly slow, traffic-heavy, three-mile journey across the city to either King's or Sidney Sussex college, with all the equipment carried in their car boots. It wasn't quite as straightforward as staying out a bit longer at a state-of-the-art Premier League training ground, where all you need is on site. However, at the Abbey you could go 'around the back', to a space stationed behind the Habbin Stand. A head tennis court was set up on one sparsely gravelled area, while there was a large grass section as well, with a goal painted on one wall. It was ideal for practising striking the ball more cleanly and accurately. I also did a lot of work on my first touch. Batchy would probably have called my first touch one of my biggest assets, but I still felt it needed to be that bit tighter and more reliable for me to compete in a quicker, far more physical environment.

The extra work certainly helped me to acclimatise better. But while I felt more confident on the ball, I still struggled to be vocal, to speak up on the pitch among lots of strong voices. As such a youngster, I found that when I tried to make a point, it was often greeted with a 'who the f*** are you?'-type response, so I mainly didn't waste my breath. I got some help on this when Roy enlisted the sports psychologist, John Porter, to come and work with us, I guess in the hope of ending our barren run. The first session was a real clear-the-air meeting, and I was shocked at the candid nature of some of the discussion.

Shaggy ripped into Jason Rees, our (soon to be deposed) captain, and said the former Wales international was not pulling his weight in midfield. It was agreed that we were defending too deep as a back three (or occasionally four), probably due to Fozzie being 33 and no longer very mobile. The defenders also had their input, accusing the front men of failing to hold the ball up well enough. As our frontline normally contained two of Martin Butler, Michael Kyd and Jamie Barnwell, all of whom were most comfortable using their pace to get in behind defenders, there may have been some truth in that as well. Whether air was cleared, or just more petty grievances and divisions created, I'm not sure. There was no instant transformation in our form, but we did get a win, at last.

John came back in for another session, this time focusing on some team-building exercises. One of them was a murder mystery scenario, where we had to work out a solution in groups of four or five. I was my team's scribe, full of suggestions and co-ordinating ideas. "Bloody hell, how come we never hear from you like this on the pitch?" said one of the older pros. It was a fair question with a simple answer. I felt more empowered in this situation because it was all about using your brain, and logic, areas where – unlike in football as yet – I considered myself on at least an equal footing.

The trick was to find some of that empowerment on the training pitch. Clearly I'd exuded confidence in this task, and I felt, for once, like I was being listened to. So from then on I figured that, even if I didn't always feel super-confident, I had to project such a feeling to start being taken seriously as a player. And that is what I tried to do. Mostly it was just in the form of calling for the ball a bit more forcefully, or loudly giving the odd helpful instruction to a team-mate. The kind of thing that comes naturally to a seasoned pro, but not so easily to a rookie, who's focusing all his energy on his own performance, trying to shine.

But while I felt my displays in training improved, this new-found attitude didn't seem to help too much on my full first-team debut, at Bristol Rovers in the Auto Windscreens Shield just before Christmas. I was given a start in behind the front two (more fashionably known as the No. 10 role these days) of Martin Butler and my youth team colleague, Mark McCammon. When I'd played for the reserves, it was invariably in that position, so I felt comfortable heading out of the dressing room.

Sadly for me, the game turned into an hour-long special edition of the TV show, *Beadle's About*. Only it wasn't Jeremy Beadle filling the Rovers midfield – I think I might have got a bit of change out of him if it had been – but Peter Beadle. Normally a striker (I remembered him signing for Spurs as a youngster), here he was in a deeper role, and every time I got near him, whether I had the ball or he did, he used all of his thickset, six foot frame to practically pick me up and throw me out of the way. Rovers were a decent side who, under a young Ian Holloway, made the play-offs in the division above us that year, and we struggled to make much headway in the game. I had little impact before my number was held up after 61 minutes, shortly after Jamie Cureton had scored the game's only goal.

I guess debuts are a bit like losing your virginity. Only with more spectators. Lots of hype. Lots of expectation. But your inexperience can be all too obvious. While you need to go through that first step in order to move on to better times, there's a high likelihood of feeling inadequate in the immediate aftermath. Or maybe that's just how it was for me (on both counts!). In the *Cambridge Evening News* the following day, the United reporter Randall Butt summed it up pretty accurately with his verdict on me: "Not ready." I couldn't argue with that. But the game had given me a clear indication of how much work I still had to do if I wanted to make a living from the game.

I got on with that work and showed enough in training over Christmas to force my way back onto the first-team bench for three straight games. And after a bright introduction in our 2-0 defeat at Barnet, I was chucked in from the start again, this time in a League match against rock bottom Doncaster at the Abbey.

It was very much a pressure game. We were expected to beat a side who would go on to be relegated, 15 points adrift with a goal difference of -83, and as we had won only two in 13 – following on from our earlier 15-match winless run – the gaffer was coming under scrutiny.

He asked me to play from the left wing and drift inside to find the same holes in behind the strikers that I had been for the ressies. But it didn't work out that way. On the occasions I managed to find pockets of space, I was over-anxious and over-ran the ball. And then, just before half-time, Donny took the lead. The atmosphere in the ground turned rather dark and Roy, with his job on the line, took me off at the break and went more direct, with three big strikers to get the ball forward to at every opportunity. We came back to win 2-1, Roy's job was safe, but I felt further away from being a first-team player than ever.

All I could do was keep plugging away in training and in the reserves for the rest of the season, which I did, playing well as we lifted the President's (or Capital League) Cup with a 2-1 win over Brentford. A late spurt of good results from the first team saw us up to a 16th-place finish in Division Three, building optimism for the following season, particularly with the average age of our team coming down to around 24. I got on for ten minutes in the final match of the campaign at Hull, but with training pitches becoming bone hard, my knees were feeling the effects of a first full season, and I really needed a break to recuperate and come back stronger.

When we did report back, I was joined in the first-team dressing room by six further graduates from my age group in the youth team. But they were all given only six-month or one-year deals and by the end of that season only one would remain. And that one, Larry McAvoy, who made a solitary League appearance, struggled with calf injuries which soon saw him out the door as well.

But it was nice to have them around for a while. It served to show me how far I'd actually come over the past year, as I watched them struggle under the pressure of stepping up, particularly in dealing with Preecey, who – although his heart was definitely in the right place – could be extremely acerbic and unforgiving in his comments during training. "Go tie a rock to that right foot and chuck yourself in the river" – with little sign of humour detectable in his voice – was just one example.

Having missed the early fitness work the year before as I was still training with the youth team, I had the chance to show off my long-distance running ability – Larry and I were comfortably at the front of all the runs around Royston golf course. I carried the momentum from that into the football sessions when they started, my ball-carrying skills to the fore (I would say dribbling, but I never really mastered the tricks and skills associated with that, I was more adept at attacking spaces than taking on defenders one-on-one). Playing as part of a front two in most of the sessions – a role I had rarely filled over the past year in youth or reserve teams, both of whom favoured a 3-5-2 system with me in behind the strikers – I was coming into deeper areas, combining well with others or driving forward myself to pick out through balls and play one-twos. Roy was clearly impressed, joking loudly, after another good piece of play: "Shame you've got no pace or you could play for England."

In the opening pre-season friendly at non-League neighbours Cambridge City, I played in a youthful second-half side, curling in my first senior goal (ok, it wasn't a competitive match, but it still felt like a landmark moment) from the edge of the box. Overall, pre-season could not have gone much better for me. I certainly announced myself as a more credible contender for regular first-team action, as evidenced by a couple of senior team-mates selecting me as their player to watch in the season preview supplement of the *Cambridge Evening News*.

Securing a place in the team, though, was still going to be tough. In Martin Butler, Michael Kyd and Trevor Benjamin, we had three impressive young strikers, while in Shaggy we had a wily old goalscorer who was always worth at least a spot on the bench. There was also my fellow youth team graduate, Mark McCammon, who had the power and pace to frighten any defence. So I had my work cut out, but I knew I offered something a bit different to all of them in my ability to drop into holes, providing a link with midfield that could help the team construct attacks. Even though I was left out of the 14-man squad after making the long trip to Torquay on a sunny opening day – where we scraped a wholly unmerited 1-0 victory – I felt sure that if I continued to perform well and offer an alternative frontline option for the gaffer, my chance would come to exorcise the memories of the last season's underwhelming appearances.

Four League games into the season, after a 2-1 home defeat by Hartlepool, it was obvious that Trev was having a hard time. Kyddie was struggling with a long-standing knee cartilage injury that unfortunately would never really go away and eventually ended his career, though he battled on for another 18 months or so. A spot was available alongside Buts up front.

We had a practice match on the Abbey and, with me and Mark

McCammon on opposite sides, it seemed like a direct shoot-out for the prize of a starting place at Chester the following evening. I showed up well and it was my name on the teamsheet when we arrived at the Deva Stadium, a day after I turned 19. I started the game well with some good movement down the sides, though I couldn't quite catch hold of a superb lofted pass from Preecey after peeling off at the back post. Our good start was rewarded by a double whammy midway through the first half. Buts was sent clear, only to be dragged back by the experienced centre-half Andy Crosby. The referee handed out a justified red card and, from the resulting free-kick, Alex Russell expertly clipped over the wall and into the bottom left corner. Lift off.

With confidence streaming through the team, Wanny extended our lead early in the second half before rounding off a comprehensive victory with a last-minute penalty. For me it was certainly a lot more enjoyable than my previous outings. Although I didn't score, I felt like I'd made a full contribution this time. The best bit was probably dropping a shoulder past David (brother of Garry) Flitcroft in midfield, evading his desperate sliding challenge to set off an attack, to which Flicker (who I was to play alongside later at Bury) responded by vowing: "I'll break your little legs if you do that again".

Being in the away dressing room afterwards, celebrating three points and feeling a real part of it, was absolutely amazing. It felt like all the wins I'd ever enjoyed in youth teams multiplied together. It was only a run-of-the-mill Division Three match played in front of not quite 2,200 supporters, but that night, as I replayed the match over and over in my head – in a vain attempt to get to sleep – I felt like I'd played in the FA Cup Final.

Where my two previous starting appearances had left me feeling unready and out of place, this time I felt like I belonged. I was still a long way from carving out a career in the game, but at least I'd started on that path. At last.

League and cup appearances to this point
3 (+3 as sub), 0 goals

6

The Champ Man Man

The next game was at home to Scarborough, a team destined to exit the League that season, never to return. We started where we left off at Chester and blitzed them early. Buts scored twice in the first ten minutes and should have had another soon after, while I fizzed one just wide of the far post. We were rampant. But then came the deluge.

Heavy rain swirled down, flooding the pitch and providing a huge leveller, as the game descended into a dogfight. Either side of half-time, the visitors scored from corners to level up the match. Preecey and I, not suited for the torrential conditions, were withdrawn at the hour mark and Boro grabbed a late winner – something that had seemed impossible 45 minutes earlier – from another set-piece.

Despite the defeat, I kept my place for the trip to high-flyers Scunthorpe four days later. Again we started impressively and opened the scoring when I slipped Buts in to chip the goalkeeper – my first assist in League football. Alas, we again showed a vulnerability to set plays – one laughably conceded when our big Dutch goalkeeper Arjan van Heusden ('Ice') picked up a clear back pass – and found ourselves on the wrong end of a 3-2 scoreline for the second successive match.

In the dressing room after the game there was a brawl, triggered by Buts criticising Ice about the backpass. The critique didn't go down too well. They flew at each other, grappling like wrestlers, and as I was sat in between them I nearly got scolded when a freshly made pot of tea was sent flying. While players tried to separate the pair of them, Roy just sat in the corner calmly, folding his glasses to put away and balling his socks. I guess he'd seen a few post-match bust-ups in his time and wasn't concerned. I think things boiled over because we'd played really well for large parts of two games in the previous few days, but ended up with nothing to show for it. Buts maybe wasn't too pleased at his goals going unrewarded either.

It was to prove the turning point in our season. Roy later said, when reviewing our promotion campaign, that he thought some of our best spells of football in the season had come in those three games (starting with Chester). But the subsequent turnarounds against Scarborough and Scunthorpe – with five of the six goals conceded from set-pieces – persuaded him that we were not big enough or strong enough to handle Division Three with that sort of line-up (which included me, Preecey, and playmaker Alex Russell – not an ounce of heft between us). So we went to a 4-3-3 with a frontline of Shaggy, Trev and Buts – all over six feet – which meant that, although we would still always try to play football, we could mix it with anyone if necessary. And we could hold our own at defensive corners.

So the next Saturday, at home to Leyton Orient, I was back on the bench, although an effervescent five-minute burst at the end saw me singled out for praise from Roy. "Does he look like he's sulking?" he said in reference to me, the comment aimed at a couple of players in the dressing room who had not made the bench, after playing in recent weeks. "No, he just wants to get back out there and show me what he can do. That's what I need in here. You can't all play every week, but I need everyone to be ready at all times." It was a small token of consolation to offset the disappointment of losing my place.

I would have to be largely content with a place on the bench until Christmas, although I was granted another three games in from the start when Trev got suspended. Nearly snapped in two by Jeff Eckhardt in a hard-fought 1-0 win at Cardiff, I recovered from a hugely swollen knee to play at Halifax, where I was denied a winner in a thrilling 3-3 draw by a fine save (Roy was not quite so generous regarding my shot: "Your turn on the edge of the box was like Kenny Dalglish, but you finished like Postman Pat"). Another monsoon ruined a 0-0 home draw with Shrewsbury, which passed without a shot in anger from either side. And then Trev returned. Back to the bench for me.

But there was better news to come soon enough, as the gaffer called me into his office to offer me a new two-year contract extension. £225 a week rising to £275 a week in the second year. I didn't hesitate to sign it. I clearly needed more time to develop – physically, above all, but also technically and tactically – in order to push for a regular game. The new contract gave me the security of knowing I would get that time.

However happy the gaffer was with my progress, though, he was also sensing a promotion charge might be on the cards. While I had earned my place in the squad and, on occasion, in the team, I perhaps still wasn't quite ready to be a genuine deputy for the established front three. So Roy opted to strengthen the squad before Christmas, bringing in forward Richard Walker on loan from Aston Villa. Walks was superb at receiving and protecting the ball, clever around the box, and at six foot was the perfect understudy for Shaggy, who, at 34, was probably expected – wrongly, as it turned out – to struggle playing regularly throughout an entire campaign.

It was hard, though, having been so involved, to find myself often left out of the 14-man squad (with only three subs, two forwards wasn't always a sensible option). Though in hindsight it's easier to be objective and recognise that Walks was two years older than me and further along in his development, at the time I was just thinking: "He's only played one League game as a sub – if he's coming here to develop for Aston Villa's benefit, why can't I just get more chances to develop, for Cambridge's benefit?" But as Walks was such a nice lad (not to mention a very good footballer), it was difficult to be bitter about it. I just had to keep working hard and trust that my time would come.

And as the reserves had been moved out of the Capital League into the Football Combination, there was consolation to be found, when left out of the first team, in some exciting second-string encounters. When Arsenal visited the Abbey, 500 or so fans made for quite an atmosphere. The Gunners were not filled with star names, but had the quality to score three times in ten minutes in the second half. We were 2-0 up before that burst, and rescued a draw thanks to a late Mark McCammon equaliser. I had a really good game and scored the second goal, sending me to sleep that night with many happy dreams.

They were to be rudely interrupted.

I woke up with a start, my heel throbbing. I couldn't get back to sleep and could do nothing to ease the pain. A long seven hours later, I reported for training and begged Ken to sort it out. After a minute to diagnose a nasty infection, he took a scalpel and cut away the problem. The throbbing had gone but now my heel was completely raw and there was no way I could recover in time for our trip to Scarborough at the weekend.

Roy was seething, accusing me of failing to report a blister before the Arsenal game. Preecey saw that my boots were a bit worn at the back and threw them in the bin. I swear to this day I did not knowingly play through anything, and I don't remember having any issues in the run-up to or during the match. But Roy was adamant and fined me a week's wages. "Don Howe (the late, great Arsenal and England coach) was asking me about you last night," he continued, still raging. "He liked what he saw. But you're not much f***** good to anyone like that, are you?" I didn't bother protesting my innocence too strongly, he wasn't in the mood. I just ordered some new boots and hoped I would heal reasonably quickly.

I was ready for our next Combination game, at Charlton the following Wednesday. It turned out to be pretty eventful, and for one player in particular it was the game of a lifetime. The hosts had a star-studded side, full of players regaining fitness for the first team's Premier League relegation battle. Clive Mendonca scored a hat-trick alongside Steve Jones up front, Matty Holmes – ex-West Ham – raided down the left, Mark Bowen and Anthony Barness were full-backs and veteran Paul Mortimer played in midfield. Topping it all off, Mortimer's partner in the middle was a certain John Barnes, in his first game for the club. His presence ensured the attendance of Charlton boss Alan Curbishley and *The Sun* newspaper. We had a very young team, in which I played on the left of a 4-3-3. Down the middle was Mark McCammon.

He absolutely ran Charlton ragged, scoring two, making two and putting together the best all-round game I'd ever seen from him. That helped us to an unlikely 5-4 victory, though some thanks should go to the Addicks' fallen hero Sasa Ilic, in goal, who looked a shadow of the player whose penalty-saving exploits sealed promotion in the play-off final nine months earlier. Ilic – who had actually been on trial with us at Cambridge before signing for Charlton in 1997 – never really recovered from losing his first-team spot midway through that season. But while one player's star was on the wane, another's was very much in the ascendant. Mark – 'Hightower' to the dressing room thanks to a passing resemblance to the *Police Academy* character – had certainly picked the right time to have the game of his life. Despite being involved at Cambridge for three years, he'd never been awarded more than non-contract status, so when Charlton naturally enquired about him after the game, they found that they could poach him without the need of a transfer fee. And so began a nomadic 15-year career, taking in Brentford, Brighton, Bristol City, Doncaster, Gillingham and Millwall, where he appeared briefly in an FA Cup Final against Manchester United. Not bad for a Division Three reserve with no contract. Whenever anyone asks me about the 'right place, right time' phenomenon, where one opportunely-timed performance shoots you to the stars, I tell them it's nonsense. A fairytale. A movie script. Players are always scouted many times, in many different situations, before a decision is made on them. Mostly that's true, and even more so in the present day with the resources devoted to scouting networks. But just occasionally, in very specific circumstances like Mark's, the dream of being plucked from obscurity to the Premier League lives on.

With the first team marching inexorably towards promotion, my own form took a bit of a slide. It was like the kind of regression I'd experienced at 14, which was similarly baffling at the time before a cause gradually revealed itself. That was my first major growth spurt, which took me from little boy to, well, slightly-bigger-but-still-quite-little boy. This was my final growth spurt, giving me a last inch-and-a-half and eventually edging me up to a shade under five foot nine. But while it was happening, I didn't have a clue.

I was struggling a bit in training, and then we played the last of our prestigious home reserve games, against a Chelsea side containing a young John Terry. I had a nightmare. I couldn't do anything right. My touch was off. I mistimed a couple of shots which could have given me an injection of confidence. Bad games happen, of course, but this felt different. It was like I'd lost co-ordination. The gaffer laid into me at the end, firing a pretty cheap shot by suggesting, in front of everyone, that I was being distracted by my 'new' girlfriend. Chelle had come to watch a couple of reserve games and had clearly caught his attention. "Must be those big tits," he said.

I didn't react at the time. I never thought that in the dressing room, after a game, was the right time to dispute things with a manager. With emotions running at fever pitch, the atmosphere was never conducive to rational, considered debate. Better to just take the bollocking, take the 'hairdryer' treatment, then seek a chat another day, when temperatures have cooled, if you have any issues. Roy actually called me in the next day. I put him straight about Chelle having been with me for two-and-a-half years, and he apologised for that. He re-assured me that I was still very much part of his plans, but that I seemed to have lost my way a bit. I agreed, but was at a loss to describe my recent malaise. We both probably thought that it was to do with my displacement from the first-team picture, and that may well have been a factor, my self-assurance knocked a bit.

It was only a few months later, when we came back for pre-season, that Roy would notice a distinct step-up in my height. My co-ordination returned. And I felt more in control of my foot placement again. Growth spurts bring about very subtle, progressive changes but, when you're going through it, it's disconcerting. And I was probably going through it later than most.

But although I was having a slightly difficult time of it, the promotion party carried on regardless, and was wrapped up on a memorable night at Spotland, Rochdale. With 20 minutes remaining and our game still goalless, the scoreboard flashed up to show Scunthorpe were losing at Halifax. If we won and the Irons didn't, we were up. I took an authorised break from my radio summariser duties to scream the message to our assistant physio, Den. Whether he or just a few hundred radio listeners heard my screeching, I don't know, but soon Shaggy was introduced, scoring two in the final ten minutes to seal the deal. I went down on to the pitch to join the players and fans in celebration, but there was something a little hollow about it all for me. As we piled into the dressing room, Roy made a point of coming over to me and saying: "This is for you as well; you played an important part in this." But I couldn't quite get on board with the sentiment.

On the buoyant journey home, when it was my turn to take the mic, I sang the trusty karaoke standard 'I'm A Believer'. But I wasn't one, really. I was delighted for the lads, a really great bunch who deserved the achievement. I was delighted we'd gone up, which meant that if I could push my way into the team the next year, I'd be playing at a higher level. And I was delighted with our bonus scheme, which was based on matchday squad appearances. It meant that although I played in only ten games (starting six), and my drive-share and room-mate Shaun Marshall played 23 full matches in goal, I got more bonus because I was an unused sub 14 times while, with only three subs, we never had a goalkeeper on the bench! But I wasn't delighted with how the season had panned out for me, overall.

Now, with the dust settled on my career, I can look back with pride at having been involved, and I'm happy to display my promotion shirt and medal at home (many players are never so lucky as to get any kind of medal). But at the time I was merely putting on a happy front. Inside I was desperate for the season to finish so I could get started on the next one.

The big one.

Though we eventually missed out on the title in a final day decider with Brentford at the Abbey, where Andy Woodman was inspired in goal for the Bees, we were thrown a Town Hall reception to commemorate our promotion. While the vol-au-vents and profiteroles were being guzzled, Preecey pulled me to one side and said that he and the gaffer had earmarked the next season as the one for me to break through. "You've done your two-year apprenticeship now," he said. "We see you playing 15 to 20 games next year."

His words were a great encouragement, and – after a celebratory lads holiday in Magaluf, where I gave everyone a good laugh by managing to pick up fake tan rather than sun cream from the beach bar, which left my hands stained brown for a couple of days – I couldn't wait for the summer break to finish. But when we came back to training, to start with there was only further disappointment. The growth spurt that had disorientated me on the ball towards the end of the previous season was now playing havoc with my body. It was struggling to adapt to my physical changes while being put through an arduous pre-season schedule.

On the first day, I pulled something in my back while sprinting up a hill. I took about two weeks to recover, but then after another week I felt something in my groin. My whole pre-season was being compromised. Fighting back into contention for a spot on the bench on the opening day at Bournemouth, I pulled a calf in the Friday morning session before we were due to leave. I had to get the bus home because Marshy had brought us in that day. The start of the season was just niggle after niggle after niggle. In the first three months of the season, I flitted on and off the bench, my sporadic appearances divided by a series of two-week absences where some muscle or other gave up on me temporarily. Seemingly unable to stay fit for more than a week, I wasn't able to show myself worthy of a shot at Division Two.

Roy dipped into the transfer market with another loanee from Aston Villa, Darren Byfield. We were finding the step up in quality challenging, amassing only 11 points from our first 13 games. Daz didn't fare too well with us either, cutting a frustrated figure on the right-hand side of our front three for three games before scarpering back to Villa Park. But while I'm sure he dismissed his brief spell at the Abbey from his mind as soon as possible, it was more memorable for me, by dint of my first introduction to him.

As he was shown round the dressing room, in standard fashion, being fed a bunch of names that he would forget within seconds, he stopped when he heard my name. "So you're Tom Youngs, then?" he said. This was a highly-rated youngster who'd made a handful of Premier League appearances. I was an obscure young player with a couple of handfuls of Division Three appearances under my belt. And he was the one recognising my name.

"I always have to sign you on *Champ Man*," he continued. In that instant I recognised the reach of the *Championship Manager* computer game. My best mate James and I had been playing it for years, and shared the excitement of my first inclusion on the 1997/98 version (though it was rather galling the first time the Tottenham team I'd chosen to manage were knocked out of the FA Cup by Nottingham Forest, thanks to two goals from me!). *Champ Man 3* had just been released and though I realised, from starting to play it, that the fictional me had pretty good stats, I didn't yet realise quite how good. Daz was telling me about him winning Champions Leagues with me starring up front for the Villa. Pretty soon I did a Q&A on the Cambridge fans' website, U's Net, where the administrator Andrea Thrussell had to edit out a bunch of duplicated questions that all amounted to the same thing – 'Do you know how good you are on *Championship Manager*?' They were sent in from all over the world – the USA, Canada, Scandinavia and many places in between.

While it was a lot of fun, particularly when I managed to flog myself for millions (my record was £16.5 million to Rangers), I did think that some people were using it to take the piss. "16 million quid? England regular? He can't even get in the Cambridge team."

I was constantly trying to remind people that it was a computer game, with no basis in real life. Yes, the game had pretty good scouting, which in more recent editions has become ever more sophisticated and accurate, but it was still no reliable indicator of future performance. Most of the times I played the game, I (the computer me) would end up playing for England alongside Dean Ashton and Tommy Smith – both of whom would go on to be Premier League regulars. A little known 17 year old, Zlatan Ibrahimović was also a pretty reliable signing from Malmö. But there were plenty of other superstars from the game who turned out to be nothing of the sort in real life (Tonton Zola Moukoko anyone? Thought not).

So it wasn't exactly foolproof. And I wanted to have a career, not to become an item of trivia. If I was to have any kind of career, let alone one as illustrious as my virtual self, I needed to shake my run of injuries and get back out on the pitch. I still hadn't even scored a goal in the Football League yet. But thankfully that was about to change.

League and cup appearances to this point
8 (+13 as sub), 0 goals

7

Making it to Teletext

October 23rd 1999. A day never to be forgotten. Tottenham beat Manchester United at White Hart Lane, which never (well, hardly ever) happened. Kanu scored that magical late hat-trick to give Arsenal a 3-2 comeback win at Chelsea. But the most important footballing event – at least to my mind, if not perhaps that of the entire country – occurred at Priestfield, the home stadium of Gillingham.

It was my second visit in six months, having watched from the stands as we beat Brighton in their temporary home on our way to promotion. The ground was much-changed though, with the main stand having been knocked down, replaced for now by eight-foot white boarding along the length of the pitch, behind the dugouts. The away end was an open terrace, which on a wet and windy day looked pretty uncomfortable.

With Trev banned, having accumulated too many yellow cards, a spot partnering Buts up front was up for grabs, with the gaffer reverting to 4-4-2. My on-off injury crisis had eased for a couple of weeks at just the right time, and Roy gave me my first start in Division Two. Gillingham were a good side, destined for promotion that year under Peter Taylor. We were fourth bottom, with two wins from 13 games.

But 17 minutes in, Neil Mustoe received the ball in midfield, looked up, and saw me darting from left to right, arcing in between the Gills' centre-halves. Barry Ashby, having not tracked my run, let out a desperate yelp of "Ade!" to his fellow defender Adrian Pennock, hoping that I could be cut off. I couldn't. Muzzie curled the ball delightfully over Pennock's head and I took it on the half-volley on the edge of the box. My first touch was perfectly weighted to evade the onrushing

Vince Bartram in goal and, from a slightly acute angle, I slotted into the net. I closed my eyes, clenched my fists, and let out a cathartic roar as I waited for my team-mates to run over. It was right in front of the away fans, who were getting soaked in their uncovered area. The considerable noise they made suggested they were glad for a reason to jump up and down and keep warm.

The goal inspired me to a busy first-half performance, in which I later made a weaving run from the left wing and skidded a low ball across the face of goal, though no-one could quite manage to apply a finishing touch. At half-time we were feeling pretty good about ourselves, but an angry Peter Taylor made two substitutions at the break. One sub, John Hodge, created two goals for the other, Andy Thomson (although a miscued punch from Ice certainly helped them with the equaliser) and the result was turned on its head by the final whistle.

Roy had brought me off, looking bedraggled and tired, after 72 minutes. With precious few minutes of football in the bank in this stop-start season, only the extra buzz of the goal kept me going that long, probably. But my adrenaline had masked another injury, this time a hamstring strain, which I was unaware of until I had a bath on the Sunday evening and felt the back of my leg tighten up. Another three weeks out was all I needed. I'd finally got my name on Teletext (Chelle took a picture of her TV to prove it!) and in the Sunday papers, and I could record my strike on *Goals On Sunday* to show to friends. But more time on the sidelines it would have to be. Roy went back into the transfer market, bringing in Steve Guinan, a 24-year-old striker from Nottingham Forest.

I managed to get another start on Boxing Day at Oxford, again in a front pairing with Buts. But a promising start was wasted when Martin McNeil got himself sent off for a second booking on the half-hour mark. A fine rearguard action followed, before we succumbed to a Matt Murphy winner with seven minutes to go. After that, our recent move to 4-4-2 meant one less striker in the squad most weeks and, with Guinan preferred, I was back in the stands for the next month.

I missed out on the excitement of our FA Cup fourth round win at Wrexham and the subsequent fifth round home tie against Bolton, playing the role of incensed fan as well as any of those around me as Trev was hauled down by Mike Whitlow when in on goal. It was a clear red card, which – with us already 1-0 up – could have helped seal a famous victory. Inexplicably, though, referee John Brandwood awarded a free-kick to Bolton. Bob Taylor and Eiður Guðjohnsen led a second-half fightback as Wanderers rather fortuitously continued their cup run, which ended at the semi-final stage.

I did get a runout in between, as part of a largely reserve team in the Auto Windscreens Shield against Barnet, managing to score my first senior goal at the Abbey thanks to a friendly deflection. We went on to lose to an extra-time golden goal, after which a livid Roy launched into the most unexpected of post-match tirades. It was not the defeat, nor the performance, which aroused his ire, but one player.

The player, who I shall leave nameless, had played a minor role in Barnet's winning goal, losing the ball somewhat casually in midfield. This was the starting point of Roy's debrief, but pretty soon it was clear that something else was at play.

"Where were you on Saturday night?" asked the gaffer.

"Nowhere, boss," came a slightly puzzled reply.

"Well, where were you?" the question came back.

We'd all been out in Cambridge to celebrate reaching the fifth round of the FA Cup. I'd spent the night at Muzzie's house in Newmarket. But this player had not been there. Again, his response was rather non-committal.

"It's a simple question: where were you?" continued Roy, edging ever nearer to the object of his inquisition.

"Nowhere," said the player. "What do you mean?"

"I'll tell you where you were," shouted a now simmering gaffer, inches from the player's face. "In the police station, that's where. And did you come and tell me about it? No, I had to hear about it from some c*** in the town. How embarrassed do you think that makes me? What impression do you think it gives of the club?"

I'd seen the gaffer upset before, but this was another level. I don't know how many of the lads knew. Not many, judging by the stunned silence afterwards. (I'm still not sure exactly what happened, though I don't think any charges ever came of it). The player was (and is) a good guy. An intelligent guy. Alcohol can do strange things to people. The episode meant that my first home goal for the first team was largely forgotten. But I didn't have to wait too long for a more memorable strike.

Bolton's visit marked the last Cambridge appearance of Buts, after 128 games and 53 goals. His departure – for a staggering £750,000 to a Reading side who, though well-set for the rapid progress that would eventually see them into the Premier League, were at this point in the Division Two relegation zone with us – meant that there was an opening in the side, or at least, initially, the matchday squad. Buts's last League game had seen us beat Chesterfield to climb above them and off the bottom of the table, but we were still five points adrift of safety with only four wins to our name all season, none away from home. With 20 games remaining, we were in a fix.

But team spirit, that much-vaunted quality, remained high. When people talk about spirit, they assume it's all about players getting on well off the pitch, but it's not. While we did get on very well, having grown as a team together over the past two or three years, that wasn't the key factor. It helped, but being good mates won't ever make you dig in and persevere if, as a group, you don't actually – at heart – fancy your chances. Belief on the pitch – in what you're being asked to do and in each other's ability and willingness to do it – is far more important than camaraderie off it. Crucially, confidence wasn't at a particularly low ebb. We'd not been played off the park many times, just beaten by a bit of extra nous or quality when it mattered. Now we just needed to provide that ourselves.

With Trev growing in stature with each passing week, I thought I might get a chance to play alongside my old youth team strike partner. Our next opponents were Wigan Athletic. Top-of-the-table Wigan Athletic. Roy went with Steve Guinan. But at least I was on the bench. I had to hope, as all substitutes do, that Steve wouldn't have the best of games, so I might get my chance. But, instead, a stroke of luck arrived in more unexpected fashion.

Not that it was lucky for everyone. With half an hour gone, Alex Russell collapsed in a heap while trying to deliver a long pass. On our five-man bench, Preecey was our only genuine midfield cover. He – and Roy – knew that an hour would be too much for him. So with few other options available, the gaffer asked if I thought I could do a job wide on the left. The same position in which I'd endured a difficult home debut against Donny two years before.

"Sure," I said, with as much conviction as possible. With a couple more years behind me, and with Clive Wilson's experience backing me up from left back, I was sure I could make a better go of it this time. I had to. First-team chances had hardly been plentiful, so weren't to be wasted. In the 15 minutes between my arrival and the interval, I was very careful, tentative even, feeling my way into the game. We were already 1-0 down to a very good side containing Arjan de Zeeuw at centre-half, Roberto Martinez in midfield, goalscoring wideman Andy Liddell and 23-goal striker Stuart Barlow, who'd opened the scoring (albeit with a mis-hit cross).

Then on the stroke of half-time, an innocuous ball rolled into Steve on the halfway line drew a completely unnecessary and rash challenge from Wigan's right-back Carl Bradshaw, who received a second yellow card. The second half became an extended attack versus defence session, with the supremely organised visitors keeping us at arm's length with relative ease. Gradually we wore them down, though, and after Steve had whistled one just wide from the edge of the box, I spied an opportunity of my own. Increasingly drifting into central areas, I anticipated correctly a trademark Trev roll as de Zeeuw got too tight, and while Trev appealed in vain for a penalty, I bisected the fallen bodies to find room for a shot. Roy Carroll spread himself well, blocking for a corner, and I feared my chance to be the hero was gone.

But we, and I, plugged away, and with seconds left in stoppage time, Carroll finally made an error, spilling Shaggy's deflected shot. Gambling on just such a mistake, I beat all defenders to the rebound, concentrated on making a firm connection, and saw the ball nestle in the bottom left corner. The ground erupted – small though the Abbey is, it can be pretty noisy in there – and, at the second time of asking, I *was* the hero.

It was only a point, and it actually saw us remain at the foot of the table, with Chesterfield having taken advantage of our cup diversion to creep back ahead. But it felt very significant. To the supporters, to the team, and of course to me personally.

When Roy had left me out of the team after my short run of games in the promotion season, he'd said that while playing well is important, when it comes to whether or not you stay in the side, particularly for an unproven youngster, "I need something to force my hand, like a goal." Well, finally I had that goal to make his mind up, and I figured it would buy me a bit more time on the pitch.

Two tricky away fixtures followed, a narrow 1-0 defeat at promotion-chasing Stoke coming before a trip to Notts County, also on the verge of the play-offs. Having missed a decent chance in the first half, slicing into the side netting, I was glancing nervously at the bench midway through the second half as a fit-again Michael Kyd started to warm up more vigorously. With us trailing 2-1, I had to do something quickly (Roy confirmed after the match that a change had been imminent). As Trev switched play to me, I pushed the ball past full-back Richard Holmes, hoping to catch him by surprise. It worked and as he tried to pull me back, I shrugged him off before smashing sweetly into the far corner with my weaker left foot. In the last minute, Trev completed our first away win since the giddy night at Rochdale ten months earlier. We were off the bottom of the table again and the great escape was on.

John Porter had come back in for a session and advised us to ignore the actual League table and create our own for the rest of the season, starting with the crunch Chesterfield game. If we could finish in the top six of our table, or maybe even the top ten, then we could stay up. Muzzie took great pride in updating the table after every week's fixtures.

I still wasn't feeling completely at home in my role as a wide midfielder. I didn't fancy my chances of flying past many full-backs on the outside like Ryan Giggs, but I was learning to adapt, reading balls into the front men and breaking into dangerous areas in front of and behind the opposition's backline. And doing what I'd always been good at, anticipating bounces and bobbles in the box and sniffing out chances to score.

This instinct brought a run of five goals in three games, starting with a brace against Bristol City at home. Next came the sweetest goal of my career, a half-volley at Scunthorpe which nestled in the stanchion, a la Trevor Brooking for England in Hungary back in the early 1980s. The lads were already slaughtering me for having a "duller celebration than Shearer" – it was a very uncontrived, spontaneous act: two arms out, looking as if I was beckoning someone to jump out of the crowd and on to me – and the fact that I hadn't made something of the ball wedging in the top corner led to more ribbing. But I didn't even know until a couple of the lads mentioned it after the game.

Finally came a couple of headers – I use the term loosely as neither hit my forehead; one cheek and one nose, I think – to put us into a 2-1 lead at home to Wrexham. We had a real off-day defensively and went on to lose 4-3, but we still had 17 points from 11 games in our special League table, having only gained the same amount from the opening 25 games. And I had nine for the season. In 12 starts.

The recent rise to prominence saw me invited to the club's Sportsman's Dinner, where fans and local businessmen could pay for the dubious privilege of having a player on their table as they wined and dined. It was one of the most embarrassing nights of my professional life. Nothing to do with my table, though. With the team enjoying a real upturn in results, the gaffer thought it would be good to have all the lads attend. For those not selected to accompany the paying guests, a players' table awaited. Not one of Roy's better ideas.

Egged on by each other, and with no outsiders to rein in their behaviour, the lads got more and more drunk as the evening went on. The guest speaker, former Nottingham Forest and Leeds striker Duncan McKenzie, was heckled and then saw balls of cheese fly past his nose. He didn't even flinch but the audience were not impressed. "Show some respect," bellowed one of them. "Come on lads, grow up," yelled another. At one point the sound system started crackling. Thankfully, it would not have been obvious to everyone that one of the lads was urinating into a speaker.

The night had started with compere Trevor Peer, the BBC Radio Cambridgeshire commentator, joking that "if you see what looks like a lost 12-year-old boy, don't worry, he does actually play for the first team and is allowed to drink," when introducing me. But it was the other lads who were acting like 12 year olds (actually, that's a bit harsh on 12 year olds). I was just glad I wasn't on their table. The chairman, Reg Smart, was naturally incandescent, seeing the club's reputation besmirched in front of supporters. We'd certainly better stay up now, I remember thinking.

Frustratingly, my season pretty much ended at that point. In the next game at Luton, after coming close to scoring a couple of times in the first half, the exertion of continually chasing Matty Taylor on his marauding runs from left-back caught up with me. I found out why players would talk of being 'snipered' if their muscle pulled while running at full pelt. It did feel as if someone had shot a pellet into my calf. Ken helped me hobble off into the dressing room, where I sat with my lower leg in ice, alongside my mate Marshy, an earlier injury victim on the night. The crowd noise at Kenilworth Road really reverberates through the dressing rooms, and we could only sit and hope – having left the field with us 2-1 in front – that none of the rumbles of excitement developed into full-blown celebration. But two minutes into stoppage time, it felt like the dressing room ceiling would collapse on us as Town fans jumped for joy at an equaliser. It was a horrible way to experience the dropping of two potentially vital points in the battle against relegation.

I missed three games with the injury, but watched

appreciatively as the boys won two of them, 2-0 against fellow strugglers Oxford on our quagmire of a pitch, and 3-0 at home to Bury, who obligingly had two men sent off before half-time. I came back mainly as a substitute thereafter, playing a few cameos as we secured the two further wins required to remain in Division Two, the second by outplaying David Moyes's champions-elect Preston on a jubilant Easter Monday at the Abbey.

I missed the chance to start that game after enduring a torrid return to the line-up at Colchester two days before. Fond memories of my reserves debut at the same ground – which had initially propelled me into the first-team picture – were quickly erased. I got no change out of the home right-back, before slicing hideously wide from six yards when poised to reduce our 2-0 deficit, just before half-time.

It was my first really bad miss at first-team level and didn't go down well with the travelling supporters behind the goal. That unique sound of deflation leading into disgust, when a crowd of fans expect a definite goal but don't get one, hits you in the pit of your stomach. You so desperately want to replay the moment, but all you can do is yearn for another chance to come along so you can put it right. There was no second chance, though, and the gaffer reverted to the team which had won three of the previous five. So it was John Hansen – rather than me – getting on the end of a cross to seal victory over Preston (in far more spectacular fashion than I could ever have managed, it has to be said). But it did the job, and we stayed up. And unlike a year earlier, when I felt very peripheral in our promotion celebrations, this time I felt like I'd played a major part.

At the end of the season, I was awarded the supporters' young player of the year, voted for on the U's Net website. They'd come up with a proper chant for me, robbing the descending tune from (I believe) a song about Andy Cole. Previously their chants had been less reverent, more humorous. "He's got no pubes but we don't care" or "Tommy, cut your hair" were the most repeated. "Tom Youngs has got A Levels" was at least more complimentary, but still didn't really infer appreciation of my actual football skills. There seemed a bit more of that in their singing now.

The framed award listed a few of the quotes from the fans who voted, my favourite being: 'a new Peter Beardsley in the making, but for his play, not for his looks!' Due to having, in Andrea, a very passionate fan in charge, the U's Net site was superbly put together and one of the most popular and well-visited fan sites in a still quite embryonic online arena, where not all clubs even yet had official sites worth looking at. As mentioned earlier, I'd done Q&As for the site, and I was a frequent visitor to the fans forum, purely out of curiosity. It didn't always make for pleasant reading. Before breaking through and scoring the goals to help us avoid relegation, the consensus was that I was too small, too weak, too injury-prone and, although there was plenty of goodwill about, even my advocates were beginning to doubt whether I'd ever make the step-up. I never needed any extra motivation to make it – I was strong-willed enough on my own – but I won't deny it was pleasing to see some of the doubters end up providing the positive comments on my award.

I always kept my distance, though. I never posted on the forum, even under a pseudonym, as I know some players did. In today's Twittersphere, full of personal abuse, I'm not sure it would be so easy to remain detached. But I found it useful to canvas fan opinion – so it was easier to chat with them in the bar, if nothing else – while also recognising that they were supporters, not professionals, so that opinion wouldn't always be particularly well-founded.

And there was plenty of unfounded nonsense online in the summer of 2000. Having finally had an impact in the first team, and probably further fuelled by my *Championship Manager* 'pedigree', supporters from Cambridge and other teams had me on the verge of moves all over the country. I'd often hear about the rumour mill second hand from friends. Liverpool, QPR, Crystal Palace, Sheffield Wednesday – someone would pluck a new prospective destination for me out of the air every week. Of course, I didn't believe a word of it. Any of it. But then a big bid came in, one that would definitely help further my prospects.

The bid wasn't for me. It was for Trev. £1.5 million from Leicester City. Trev had finished the season with 20 League goals and I was delighted for him, even though most of us were wondering how he would get on in training with Premier League players. An impressive physical specimen, he was still pretty raw technically. But, regardless, his move, and hefty price tag, was clear evidence that top clubs were still prepared to have a look at players from lower down the League ladder. Which gave hope to the rest of us. And Trev's departure meant another vacated spot for a striker in the squad. Despite success playing on the wing over the previous few months, I was still confident that I could offer more in a central forward role.

Before finding out whether Roy agreed with that, though, came other matters. I was handed an envelope in pre-season. In recognition of my progress over the previous year, and in light of establishing myself as an important member of the first-team squad, it was a new contract offer. I opened it with nervous anticipation.

I was to be disappointed.

League and cup appearances to this point
20 (+20 as sub), 9 goals

8

From Purple Patch to Blue Monday

The two-year extension on offer had a standard £50 rise per week in each year. The same increment as between my first and second contracts. But during that period, I'd played only a few games, with little lasting impact. Now I'd been playing regularly and having a real influence. Scoring goals that brought us points as we strove to stay in a league that our attendances and wage bill suggested should be beyond us. We had players on two, even three times the £325 a week I was offered. And that didn't quite sit right with me. I was never motivated by money, but playing football was still a job, not a hobby, and in any job you want to be paid fairly compared to colleagues, according to your contribution.

I didn't really feel comfortable arguing the toss with Roy, as I felt sure he would try to put me in my place and re-iterate that I was still far from a finished article. I didn't want to come across as a 'big-time Charlie', convinced of my own significance thanks to a few months of relative success. I didn't think I was being one; I thought my opinion was rational. But I didn't want to risk antagonising the man who, by selecting me in his team or not, could effectively hold my career – at such a key stage in its development – in his hands.

I'd had a few phone calls from agents touting for my business, and I thought it might be time to consider hiring one. I felt that bringing in a third party would eradicate, or at least greatly reduce, the chance of a personal stand-off with the manager. I was also thinking of a potential day in the future when I might have to sit in front of Sir Alex Ferguson (real delusions of grandeur now, I realise) and know what to ask for. I thought I could do with some help in that situation, should it ever arise.

The trouble with the agents (or more often their minions) that did call me was that they never talked about me personally, or about having seen me play. Or about football, very much. From some of them I got the impression they'd only heard of me third-hand, from others in the game, and knew little about how or where I played. The discussions were always about other players that they worked with and how they'd helped them to the top, about investments they could help me with in the future, or about boot deals. I didn't really care about those things. I could look after my own finances. I was just fine ordering my boots through the club. And I was pretty sure only consistently good performances could get me a move to the top. Not an agent. An agent with good contacts could help smooth the process and get a great deal, but they couldn't persuade a top manager to buy a player he or his scouts didn't rate. All I wanted was someone who could negotiate the best contract on my behalf when necessary. Nothing more.

Richard Cody introduced himself in the club bar after our pre-season game with Norwich. There was no mention of investments. Or boots (though he did have a deal with Valsport, my favourite bootmaker, which was a nice surprise when I found out later). He just talked about watching me the previous season, naming scouts he'd sat with and discussed me with. And what they'd said about me, good and bad. "Finds time and space well": good. "Inconsistent": not so good. We went for a coffee the following week, as the season got underway, and had a longer chat. A couple of weeks later he came round to my house to see Mum. I enlisted his help on my recent contract offer as a trial.

By this point, the League campaign was in full flow, and we were making a decent enough fist of it. The first four games had brought a desperately disappointing home defeat to Bury, a creditable draw at Bournemouth and two slightly streaky 1-0 wins, at Notts County and at home to Bristol City. With three new forwards brought in, I'd been stationed on the left or right wing in three of those games, and on the bench in Nottingham. I was solid but distinctly unspectacular. I was still craving a chance up front, particularly as I felt I complemented one of our new signings, Zema Abbey – strong, quick, powerful in the air but with a deft touch – pretty well.

I got my wish to play with Zema at Oxford in our next game, and we combined well. He nodded a long pass down, allowing me a clear run on goal, and I slid my first of the season into the corner. But despite a solid haul of eight points from our first five games, the team wasn't functioning particularly well. While I was delighted to get a chance up top, it left us with a surfeit of central midfielders filling the four slots in our midfield. We lacked a bit of balance. So it was no great surprise when I was back out on the right for our next League game, at home to Rotherham. And what a day it turned out to be.

We were 1-0 down to an early Mark Robins header, but once Ian Ashbee had charged forward to equalise, we blew the Millers away. I unleashed an unusually venomous strike which crashed in off the bar to make it 3-1 before half-time, and rounded off proceedings with a close range finish for our sixth (that's right, sixth) of the afternoon. "Two goals from midfield, hey? That'll get people coming along to watch you," the gaffer commented in the dressing room. Stubbornly refusing to concede that I should be seen as a midfielder rather than a forward, I quickly pointed out that the second goal had actually come when I'd moved up front after a substitution. On the Tuesday we followed up that comprehensive win with another demolition job, scoring four without reply against Port Vale. My goal, a sweetly-struck half-volley, came courtesy of another Zema knockdown.

We encountered a blip in our next game against Bristol Rovers, though it was more closely contested than the 3-0 scoreline suggests. After the game, Preecey had a pop at me for not protecting myself enough.

Roy had sometimes used me as an example to the younger players, highlighting my bravery despite my small, slight stature. "I'd back him in a tackle against anyone," he'd say. Although I'm sure no-one would remember me as a tackler, I never did shy away from a full-blooded challenge. My favourite one had come in a League Cup tie against Portsmouth a few weeks earlier. A real bone-cruncher with Justin Edinburgh, renowned as a pretty fierce defender and someone I used to cheer on at Spurs. But Preecey – who, standing at five foot six, knew all about being diminutive on the pitch – thought sometimes I was too brave. Needlessly brave.

Against Rovers, I went in somewhat suicidally to take the ball on my chest, stooping low as boots were flying in. I thought I could burst through the midfield line, but just ended up with a hefty whack to my right hip, which left me badly bruised and compromised my movement for the rest of the time I was on the pitch. I refused to flag up my injury because I thought I could play through it, until Preecey noticed me struggling early in the second half and instructed Roy to bring me off. "There's no point in being a soldier all the time," he said. "If you can't play, you're no good to us. We'd rather bring someone else on who's ready to go. And you need to learn when to stay out of things. If it's not going to score us a goal, or save us a goal, what's the point of getting yourself hurt?"

I'd probably always wanted to show conspicuous physical bravery, right from my early days at Cambridge, because I assumed everyone would look at me – baby-faced little lad with bony knees – and expect me to be a weak, namby-pamby player. And associate that with mental weakness, which would count against me. So I did make a conscious effort to put myself about where possible. Preecey certainly had a point, though.

Despite the defeat, we were still full of confidence, and rattled off another couple of wins. At Oldham, once Roy abandoned an ill-fated attempt at playing 3-5-2 after an awkward first half-hour, we ran out comfortable winners. I got things started when the ball broke for me 40 yards out and, as the home defence parted helpfully, I ghosted through and dinked gently over the advancing Gary Kelly. On the hour mark, I added another, anticipating a ricochet better than the Oldham back four and rounding Kelly to slot home.

Even better, on a personal level, was the next game against

struggling Luton. It was a Friday night match, and thanks to my recent run of six goals in six games, *BBC Look East* had decided to do a profile on me, to air before the game that evening. Ever looking for an interesting angle, they'd heard from our press officer Graham that I played the piano (that's putting it a bit strongly; I would noodle around a bit, making up little tunes or trying to pick up, by ear, any songs I liked at the time), so they came round to my house to film me playing 'Trouble' by Coldplay.

Sat in the dressing room with the boys listening to the team talk, I knew the programme would be on and I was just hoping that the gaffer would waffle on long enough for my two-minute segment to be finished. Once the gaffer had stopped talking, a youth team lad spilt the beans, having heard about it from Graham. But try as Shaggy might, by the time he'd switched on the TV I was nowhere to be seen. Embarrassment avoided. Phew. Now on with business.

The team endured a slovenly first half, going 1-0 down, but I'd still had enough joy to know I could make the difference in the second half. I equalised by beating the goalkeeper to John Dreyer's nicely flighted forward pass, then created the winner by slipping down the left channel and firing in a shot that was too hot to hold, allowing Zema a tap-in. Both managers were effusive in their praise of me after the game, and I'd exacted a bit of revenge on Matty Taylor – for his (entirely innocent) part in my calf injury a few months before – by giving him a tough evening. With a quarter of the season gone, we were fifth in the table with one or two games in hand on those above us.

Rich had been working with the club on my contract over the previous few weeks. He'd come to an agreement on the heads of terms (£550 a week with some added extras like a share of any transfer fee over £100,000 and a loyalty bonus if I was still at Cambridge at the end of each season – things I would have never thought to ask for on my own), but at the last minute the club threw a spanner in the works. Whereas the previous contract offer was scheduled to start from the first day of the season, the new, improved (and in my mind, fair and realistic) offer was no longer to be backdated and would only start once signed. Rich wasn't happy with this revision and said he wanted more time to work with the club. I was happy with that, but a week after the Luton game, on the eve of our trip to Colchester, the club played hardball.

After training, Roy informed me and Marshy – who'd also been negotiating a new deal – that he would not be able to select us until we agreed to sign. It seemed like the club had guessed – quite rightly, as it turned out – that Rich would not be able to suddenly drop everything and make an appearance in Cambridge late on a Friday. Thus leaving two 21 year olds in a difficult, pressure-cooker situation that would likely end in contracts being signed with no amendments needed.

I spoke to Rich on the phone, outlining the situation, and he said he'd speak to the club and get back to me. A couple of hours later – it was gone six o'clock by this stage – the return call came and the club had refused to budge. Marshy and I were called into a meeting with the chairman who made it clear that the club was in charge, and that the contract on the table needed to be signed.

I called Rich back one last time, and he could sense that I just wanted to put an end to the matter, get home and prepare for the next day's game.

"You'd rather just sign the contract, wouldn't you?" he asked.

"Yes," I said.

"Well, you should sign it," continued Rich. "I'm not happy with it, or how it's been done, but I don't want you getting stressed and stuck at the club like this with a game tomorrow."

I spoke to Marshy, and he was of the same mind. So we went back to see the chairman.

Having agreed to sign, the pens were just being readied when, out of nowhere, Marshy started mouthing off at the chairman, telling him that this was not how business should be done; that he didn't like the goalposts being moved, or having a gun held to his head; and that it was a poor way to treat lads who'd been on the club's books for years. I just sat there in stunned silence.

Initially, Mr Smart appeared affronted. "Do you know how

many times I've sat here and the goalposts have been moved on me by players and their agents?" he started angrily, before listing a few examples. But after a few minutes, he made an abrupt about-turn, just as unexpected as Marshy's outburst. "Oh, just give them the backpay," he proclaimed.

Quite how Marshy's words changed his mind, I'm not sure. But I wasn't complaining. The best part of the episode was that to Marshy – who'd only been on the bench since the summer arrival of Lionel Perez, and whose deal was structured differently – the issue was only worth about a couple of hundred quid. For me it was worth nearly two grand. I'd have happily foregone that to put it all to bed, as all I cared about was not losing my place in the team. Marshy didn't have that to worry about, so perhaps he was emboldened to speak up. In any case, I owed him a drink, as Pinch, the club secretary, was quick to point out once the chairman had left. I got home at about nine o'clock.

The game at Colchester was ruined by Tom Cowan getting himself sent off in the first 20 minutes, and I barely got a kick. But on the Tuesday, desperate to make up for having missed out at Colchester, I had probably my best game for Cambridge. It was a local derby with Northampton, who took an early two-goal lead through a Jamie Forrester double, the second a quite ridiculous long-range strike. But before, during and particularly after Jamie's brace, I was like a man possessed. I think I had seven shots on target in the match and created countless chances for others. Rather devastatingly, only one of my efforts – and none of anyone else's – found the back of the net, thanks to a superb performance from Keith Wright in goal and a valiant defensive performance from The Cobblers.

But despite an unjust defeat, which dropped us down to ninth in the table, my self-belief was at an all-time high. Eight goals in ten games. From midfield, mainly (however much I may have tried try to deny it). I was playing well, finding space 'between the lines' (to use a footballing cliché) and picking good times to make penetrative forward runs. I thought I, and the team, was poised for great things in the campaign. But something else had happened that night which was soon to pour cold water on my optimism.

Before the game, before even the team-talk had started properly, Roy asked Zema if he was going to sign the contract on offer to him from the club. Zema – who'd joined us a few months earlier from non-League Hitchin – said no. At which point Roy asked him to leave the dressing room and replaced him in the starting line-up with Shaggy. On that particular night, the change didn't affect us greatly, and certainly had nothing to do with the outcome. But over the coming weeks and months, the importance of Zema – who would play only three further games for Cambridge before his stand-off brought a £350,000 move to Norwich – became abundantly clear to anyone who had not been aware of it.

The key to this importance was all the work he did outside the box. If the team was under the cosh, he could turn any ball forward – even the ugliest, most uncultured clearance – into something worthwhile. Ball smashed over the top? He was quick enough to work the channels and put defenders under pressure. Goal kicks and lofted clearances? He was rarely beaten in the air. When balls were clipped forward with good intentions, but a bit imprecisely (as many are in Division Two), he was the best I've seen at leaping to take the ball on his chest in mid-air, managing to keep the ball both under control and out of the reach of his markers. And he was as reliable as anyone I've played with at holding the ball up – defenders just could not get around him, even after he'd shaved off his dreadlocks and they'd stopped thwacking people in the face. All of this made him the perfect target man for me to base my play around, whether up top with him or – more often – joining from wide.

Probably the only thing letting Zema down at this stage was his finishing, which was the weakest part of his game. He didn't look like becoming a prolific goalscorer. But that didn't really matter. Many Liverpool and England fans constantly questioned why Emile Heskey was regularly picked as a striker, when his goals to games ratio was far from brilliant. But it was what his presence enabled those around him to do that made him so indispensable. It's why Michael Owen loved playing –

and scored bucket-loads – alongside him. Of course it would always be preferable – even more so at the very highest level – to have someone who combined those outside-the-box qualities with a sure touch in front of goal. But as they're not exactly ten-a-penny, any manager has to do what he can to get the best out of the squad available to him. And if a striker isn't prolific – though Zema would certainly have chipped in with a few – but brings the best out of team-mates who can contribute enough goals to compensate, he can become vital. Clearly Norwich felt Zema could help knit their team together as he had done ours.

His departure left a gaping hole in our squad. When you're operating with a budget as restricted as Cambridge's was at that time, replacing significant players when they move on – so as to cause minimum disruption to the team's way of playing – is almost impossible. Shaggy was still game and a fine player, but at 36 obviously could not come close to providing the same athleticism. Roy brought in Paul Connor on loan from Stoke. 'Trig' (standard *Only Fools and Horses*-inspired dressing room nickname for anyone deemed a bit slow on the uptake) was technically good, an accomplished finisher, and I got on with him really well. But though he was six foot tall, he was skinnier than me and had about as much physical presence.

I switched regularly between playing on the wing and up front with Trig over the coming weeks, and we linked up cleverly at times. He scored five in 12. But with no real pace or power between us – Trig was quicker than me but by no means rapid – everything had to be perfect and precise if it was to come off. There was no longer an easy 'out' for the team as there had been with Zema. Everything came under more scrutiny. Finding it harder to relieve pressure, the back four lauded as 'experienced' early in the campaign were now being decried as 'old'. Ash and Wanny in midfield went from being a 'solid screen' to being 'too similar' in the eyes of some fans and commentators.

If I seem to be overplaying the importance of one player, I make no apologies for it. In the current climate of increased statistical analysis (which I'm all for, by the way), where individual players are rated on every single action as detailed by

Opta and Prozone, the relationships *between* players sometimes seem to be forgotten. It is a team game, after all.

If a striker's strength is in running behind defences, but his team doesn't contain a player or players capable of seeing those runs and finding them, he may look unproductive and struggle to score goals. Stick him in a different side, with a supplier on his wavelength, and he might suddenly score freely. Similarly an excellent passer needs runners and targets to display his talent and create chances and make assists. Without them, he may end up with poor creative stats and find himself derided for lacking defensive qualities. In a different team, he may be hailed as a superb playmaker with tons of assists. No-one will care anymore that he can't tackle.

Players make connections with each other over time, which can greatly improve their mutual performance. At Cambridge, when I played up front, I had a great affinity with Alex Russell, when he was fit. We were constantly making eye contact and I knew if I made a run, he'd spot it. When I was playing wide, Trev and Zema were perfect foils for me because not only were they reliable at keeping the ball away from defenders, but I could read which way they were going to turn when they held the ball up and time my runs accordingly. Which helped me score plenty of the 19 goals I managed to bag in the calendar year 2000. Those sorts of connections can have a huge influence on the effectiveness of both players. And particularly for a player, like me, not capable of the individualism to turn a game without help, they could be the difference between looking brilliant or ineffective.

At times in the 13-game winless run that followed Zema's departure, I did struggle to get into games as much as before. I wasn't playing badly, as such, but the same opportunities were not always coming because our patterns of play were, obviously, not the same. And when things aren't coming easily, you sometimes start to force the issue. I found myself trying to do things that weren't really on, when I just needed to keep doing what I was good at.

In the midst of our difficult spell, during which we'd already conceded one stoppage-time equaliser, against Brentford, things came to a head when we lost a three-goal lead in the last 14 minutes at home to lowly Swansea. Even though we'd played really well for three-quarters of the match, Swansea's first goal exposed our fragile confidence, and anxiety crept in. Suddenly we stopped playing normally, unsure whether to just retain possession or keep going forward when the chance arose. We couldn't get out. And two more goals for Swansea in the final two minutes sealed a pretty humiliating draw.

More humiliation nearly befell Muzzie on the Monday, when we analysed a video of the game with the gaffer and Preecey. About five minutes after half-time, Muzzie had missed a sitter to put us out of sight at 4-0. On his way back to the halfway line, with our seemingly comfortable lead ensuring spirits were high, he mocked himself by gesturing as if to flush an imaginary toilet for the lads. All the boys knew this moment was coming on the tape, and were wincing at the thought of Roy and Preecey seeing it. Just in time, Preecey grabbed the remote and pushed fast forward, keen to move past the good parts of our display to the abject last 15 minutes. In other circumstances, we would have been gagging for Muzzie to be rumbled and witness the gaffer's reaction, everyone ready to crack up. But not when we were stuck in a rut, unable to buy a win.

A couple of weeks later we travelled to Conference side Morecambe in the FA Cup. It was the featured game on *Match of the Day*. After giving away a free-kick from which Morecambe scored after five minutes, I redeemed myself with a crisply taken equaliser. But in wet and windy conditions, we huffed and puffed to no great effect before Mark Quayle – a striker who'd been on trial with us from Everton a year before – converted a loose ball to win the tie. Two divisions above our opponents, we were the slain giants. I had a few phone calls from friends congratulating me for scoring on *Match of the Day*. "Did you not see the score?" I asked them. I know they were just trying to be nice, but I couldn't really feel too much pleasure at the goal, given its embarrassing context.

We finally got three points again on Boxing Day, at home to

Wycombe. I played up front and had an awful first half. But some simple words from Preecey at half-time – "why haven't you been turning and running with the ball for us? You're good at that. Much better than your passing, judging by today so far" – helped me. As so often happens when confidence is low, I'd been concentrating so hard on trying to get hold of the ball and not give away possession, I was missing opportunities to do anything more expansive. Preecey was right.

So first ball into me after the break, I didn't just settle for trying to find a secure lay-off, I turned a defender and carried the ball forward. The second half went well, and I scored the winner, stabbing home a loose ball following a cross. There were lots of huge sighs of relief, from players and fans alike, in the bar after the game. After my 11th of the season, in 25 games – 17 out wide and eight up front – I felt rejuvenated and ready to go on and get 20. But that feeling lasted about three days.

We were due to play at home on the Saturday. I fell violently ill on the Friday night. The game was postponed, but I was still in no fit state for our trip to Bristol City on New Year's Day. I was rarely sick, and this was nothing like I'd ever experienced before. The doctor said it must have been a rare strain of flu, as I, like all the players, had been given a flu jab a few weeks earlier. Feeling marginally better by Wednesday 3rd, I went into the club. But Roy took one look at me and ordered me out again. "You look like sh*t," he said. "Do you want everyone to get it, whatever it is? Go home and don't come back until you really do feel better."

The following Monday, I came back in, over half a stone lighter. Starting a little under 11 stone, I didn't really have it to lose. A few days of gentle training later, and keen to get back on the pitch, I said I was ok for Saturday's game with Notts County. After a 20-minute introduction in the 2-2 draw, Roy wanted me back in from the start on the Tuesday at home to Bournemouth. I didn't want to argue, so I didn't. But that was stupid.

I was still undercooked and even only 20 minutes on the Saturday had left me completely drained. Going out against

Bournemouth, I was so weak I could hardly muster a sprint. A horrid evening for me was rather better for an 18-year-old striker in the opposition. "We've got Jermain Defoe, he's scored ten in a row," sang the visiting supporters after the forward had broken a post-war record by scoring in ten consecutive League games. The visitors won 2-0 despite being reduced to ten men before the half-hour mark. We could not shake our slump.

A couple of weeks later, I was slowly starting to feel human again, and scored a clinching second goal in a 2-0 win at Wycombe. But two games later, as we lost 1-0 at home to Swindon and dropped to 18th in the table, I strained a muscle in the back of my knee. That left me listening, helpless, at home on the radio as we suffered further defeats away to Port Vale and Bristol Rovers, two sides below us. As the final whistle neared in the latter game, commentator Trevor Peer sounded an ominous warning, hinting strongly what we all suspected, that Roy was to be relieved of his duties and replaced with John Beck, the rather infamous manager of Cambridge's past, renowned for his teams' direct football. "Be very afraid," intoned Trevor. I felt physically sick.

Roy's departure was confirmed on Monday morning when he came in to say his farewells. He was fighting back tears. All (or the vast majority) of the lads felt just as sad. For me, he was the man who'd picked me out at 17 and given me the chance and the belief to become a professional. I was gutted. But no matter how hard it was, I would have to agree, reluctantly but objectively, that it was time for him to go.

I think, by the end, the lads were so aware of the pressure mounting on Roy, so aware that any mistake could see him lose his job, that our play became stilted and anxious, paralysed even. More so than normal when wins are thin on the ground. It was the polar opposite of a manager losing the dressing room. Roy had brought in every single one of the first-team squad, either from another club or, as in my case, from the youth ranks. And we loved working for him. He commanded respect and could be firm but was always approachable. He'd led us up into League One, helped us stay there against the odds and had seemed to be setting us up for further progress before Zema-gate. We didn't want him to go. But we couldn't save him. I felt distraught that I'd only been able to play such a minimal role in his final two months.

I popped into the city that afternoon before the squad went out together to drown our sorrows, and I ran into a United fan. "Shame about Roy," he said. "But the General's coming back, he'll sort it all out." The fans seemed to be very divided on whether the return of the club's most successful manager was a good thing. Some recalled the promotions and the cup runs. Some only the grass grown long in the corners and the 'long ball' stigma. But when the boys reported to the ground the next morning, the General was indeed back in charge.

League and cup appearances to this point
49 (+24 as sub), 21 goals

9

The General

On John's first day, each player was given a timeslot for an intimate meeting with the new manager and his imposing assistant Shane Westley. As I was receiving treatment for a knee injury, I was one of the last to be summoned, so I had plenty of time to run through hypothetical conversations in my head before my time arrived. In none of them did I anticipate John's opening gambit. "Do you know what proactive means?" he asked.

I felt like Eddie Murphy's character in *Trading Places*, the homeless Billy Valentine who is taken in by the stock-trading giants the Duke brothers for a bet. When trying to offer Valentine a quick summation of how their business works, the Dukes feel the need to explain the concept of oranges. Murphy shoots a wry look to camera, as if to say "Really?" With no camera in tow, I just absorbed the insult to my intelligence and settled for a simple "Yes".

"Well, do you think your agent has been proactive enough this year?" came the follow-up question. "You're 21 and you've been scoring regularly." I replied that Rich had informed me of discussions he'd had with the scouts of some Division One clubs who had indicated a tentative interest in me (Norwich, Sheffield Wednesday and Crystal Palace, among others), and that I was sure he would be doing anything he could to firm up that interest. But also that after suffering with illness and injury in the last two months, I expected to have dropped down the pecking order with any potential suitors and just needed to get back on the pitch to restate my claims.

The rest of the meeting drifted along, past that initial topic and on to the questions all players would have been asked, about why the side has been struggling and so on. But on leaving the room, the overall message seemed quite clear: "You're our most saleable asset and we want to cash it in."

In the coming weeks that impression was confirmed by John telling me he'd spoken to Notts County and Cardiff about me, asking whether I would be interested in talking to those clubs. I'd chatted with the Notts County chief scout in our bar before, but they'd been struggling in Division Two just like Cambridge. Cardiff were in the league below and even though they appeared to be on an upward trajectory, with Sam Hammam and plenty of cash involved, there was no guarantee they would be promoted and they seemed a riskier alternative to the higher-level clubs mentioned before. So my answer was no.

As transfer deadline day came around (the traditional, old deadline day of the third Thursday in March), I'd regained fitness and played in a couple of games. After training, I had just got home when Rich called. Norwich had come in for me and he was trying to sort out a deal. They wanted to take me on loan for the rest of the season with a view to permanent deal in the summer. I was really excited. Norwich was where I wanted to go above all other clubs (at least those outside the Premier League). Dad used to take me and my brother, a Canaries fan, to Norwich all the time and I really liked the ground and its atmosphere. I'd always been impressed by the club and its set-up. I loved the city and knew it well. Plus Zema was there (although he'd already picked up the first of many nasty injuries that would befall him), and we had worked together really well on the pitch at Cambridge. I couldn't just sit at home waiting to hear of any news, so I went out music shopping for an hour.

The chance of a move to Carrow Road was not a bolt from the blue. I knew they had been to watch me a few times, and when, after that awkward first meeting with Mr Beck, I had confided in Shaggy, he'd said that he knew Norwich were keen and he would have a word with his contacts there to see if he could fix something up. So I was hopeful as I flicked through the racks in Andy's Records that afternoon.

But when I got home, with three o'clock fast approaching –

the time by which I figured anything would need to be agreed in order for me to make the trip to Norwich and finalise matters – my dream move seemed increasingly unlikely. I called Rich and he duly informed me that the clubs could not come to an agreement.

It was probably understandable from both sides. If Cambridge – who had already signed five players on a busy day – were not going to get a permanent transfer, I'm sure they would have been after some pretty strong guarantees on any eventual deal, which would have allowed them to feel more confident in signing further players for the battle against relegation. Norwich, on the other hand, probably fancied a closer look at me before committing what would could have been a sizeable fee, particularly as I had not played too much since Christmas. So logically, I was not too surprised. Emotionally, I was on the floor. Devastated.

But there was no time to wallow in disappointment. We were in the midst of a relegation battle. And if I wasn't going to be a Division One player, I certainly didn't want to be a Division Three player in a couple of months' time.

I had recovered from my minor knee injury within a week or so of Becky taking over as manager. In pretty much my first full training session back, John and Shane were trying to assess the squad's fitness levels and we did some 12-minute runs. As is typical with footballers, most of the lads were coasting along, running well within themselves, guessing that the runs would be repeated in a few weeks to gauge the effects of John's methods. Better leave a bit of room to show some progression was the school of thought. Not for me.

I was pretty sure, based on both my first meeting with John and having seen his sides play in the past, that I did not exactly fit his ideal template for an attacking player. John's successful sides (and boy was his previous Cambridge side successful) relied on repetition of tried and trusted patterns of play – balls into corners behind the opposition's backline, hemming them in to prevent clearances, winning set-pieces, building pressure. As a forward player in that team, your job is simple. You know where the ball is going to go and you make your run accordingly. My problem was that the defenders knew where the ball was going to go as well. That's not such a problem if you have power and at least a bit of pace, like Dion Dublin back in Cambridge's halcyon era of the early 1990s. Even if the defender reads the situation (how could he not?) and steals a march on you, you can either out-pace or out-muscle him to make it yours. I did not really have either of those options.

I had to rely on unpredictability in my play – will he show to feet or go in behind, or will he drop into the hole? – to engineer space for myself. The unrelenting predictability of John's tactics could be very effective with the right personnel, but it did not suit me. So I thought it was highly likely I would find myself surplus to requirements sooner or later, if he did not manage to ship me out. But I didn't want to make it easy for him.

So on the 12-minute runs, I hared round Coldham's Common (the public rec next to the old astroturf; one of our less salubrious training grounds), lapping team-mates and showing off one of my biggest strengths: my stamina. I wanted to take every opportunity to impress, because even if I was very unsure of how well I would be able to function within John's team, I would still rather be trying to make the best of it out on the pitch than stewing on the bench.

And I did try to make the best of it. In the win at Stoke and the defeat – after a late capitulation – at local rivals Peterborough, I had some good moments, including a scrappy 13th goal of the season in the latter. But in the intervening games against Oxford and high-flying Reading, although we picked up four vital points, I was in the margins and frustrated. So it wasn't a great shock when I was named as substitute for the next game at Northampton.

Becky's new signings from non-League were paired up front – Marcus Richardson and Dave Kitson. They were complete opposites. Marcus had all the power and pace required for our system, and what he lacked in technical ability he made up for in raw, infectious enthusiasm. He'd come on and scored the winner at Stoke, out-running the defence and coolly rounding the goalkeeper before seeming to blow it all by scuffing a half-hit shot towards the open net. Wayne Thomas comfortably recovered in time to clear, but swung and missed and Marcus celebrated his first League goal gleefully.

Kits was something more special. I had never seen anyone as two-footed, particularly without any grounding at a professional club. While he wasn't particularly quick, he wasn't slow either with his rangy strides, and his long legs seemed to be telescopic when stretching to get on the end of things. Throw in his aerial ability and he fitted the bill pretty well too.

They did a decent job in a comfortable 2-0 win, in which I played a small part at the end. In the next two games, against champions-elect Millwall and mid-table Brentford, I reprised my role as substitute, and scored on both occasions. While the first was pretty inconsequential in a 5-1 defeat, the second proved crucial as the platform for an unlikely late recovery to draw 2-2 and climb out of the bottom four.

Becky called me and Kits (who had set up my goal) 'gems' on a Sky Sports News interview after the game, which I found somewhat hilarious, and I earned my starting place back against Wigan the following Saturday. But an awkward fall midway through the first half left my right ankle the size of a cricket ball and my season was prematurely over. Happily, the boys pulled through in our agonising penultimate game against Colchester, and we – and I – were to remain Division Two footballers for the time being.

At the end of the season there was another round of meetings with the boss and Shane. In mine they told me that they would give me a personal programme to make me bigger, stronger and faster. "We're going to make you a two million-pound striker," John said. I did my best to ruin that prediction within a few days by coming a cropper on a scooter on our team holiday in Ayia Napa.

Thinking about it still makes me feel anxious and physically sick to this day. All the boys got scooters on our arrival, as apparently it was "the only way to get around Napa". I didn't trust myself to ride one, so I said I'd chip in with Marc Joseph –

or Jerry as he was known due to his curly hair as a youngster – if he was happy to give me a lift to wherever we needed to meet up throughout the week. That was fine until we got down to the water park early one day and the lads were nowhere to be seen. While we waited, and with an empty car park in front of us, I was tempted to have a little go on the scooter alone. Not a great idea.

My initial reluctance to rent one was well-founded. I was completely surprised by the power of what looked like a mobile hairdryer and within 20 yards I'd lost my balance. Swinging wildly from side to side, I gripped the handlebars as I desperately tried to regain control, and inadvertently added more revs. The extra burst of speed proved too much, and I crashed to the ground, with both the scooter and my legs being dragged across concrete at some speed. I am so lucky that all I ended up with was a few reasonably minor scrapes and scars (still visible 14 years later), and a £50 repair charge for the scooter.

Once I'd been patched up by the first-aiders in the water park, the lads, who had now arrived, had a good laugh at my expense. I think Jerry was the only one who didn't find it funny. He was probably as scared as me as he watched on helplessly. In my strait-laced, goody two-shoes life, it was by far the most stupid thing I have ever done.

Back in England, we were given only a week off before pre-season training began – three days a week from the back end of May to mid-June, then full-time. Sky came and did a piece showing that we were in the gym while most other footballers were enjoying their close-season break. It was the start of my new regime. Project 'Bigger, Stronger, Faster'.

Creatine was the first ingredient. I had to have it in the form of a drink three times a day, with breakfast and dinner and then before bed. No matter what flavouring was used to disguise it, it was pretty disgusting. But I went with it.

Then came the weight-training. Shane would personally oversee our use of weights, making sure we were always teetering right on the edge of our capabilities. Push it to the maximum and then a bit beyond. Power-building. Again, I went with it. I was 21, and if the manager says he's going to make you a two million-pound player, you go with it. And aside from that, I wanted to stay in the first team, and only by keeping John happy was that going to happen.

By the end of June, while 'faster' would have to wait until we started training with footballs again, there was no doubt about 'bigger' or 'stronger'. I'd put on 11 pounds in five-and-a-half weeks. Two pounds per week for five-and-a-half weeks. From 10st 13lbs to 11st 10lbs.

I'd had a bit of extra encouragement during all the exertion. Preecey had not yet negotiated his exit from the club, so he was in with us at times, and on one of his visits he said he might be able to engineer a move for me. He had foreseen the difficulties I might have under Becky, and having worked hard with me over the previous three years to improve me as a player, he didn't want to see that work go to waste. So he had recommended me to Neil Warnock, the Sheffield United manager, who was after someone who could get him goals in the Championship. Neil had told him that there was a potential move for Paul Peschisolido in the pipeline, but that nothing was certain and if it fell through, I would be his next option. To be completely honest, the prospect filled me almost as much with trepidation – given Warnock's somewhat fearsome reputation – as enthusiasm, but Preecey assured me that Neil is very supportive of his signings and would be good for me, and the prospect of testing myself a league up at a big club was exciting.

Soon came a double disappointment, though. Peschisolido sealed his move to Bramall Lane, and before I'd had the chance to really put my new physique through its paces on the training pitch, the constant weight-training at such a demanding level took its toll.

By this point we'd decamped to an army barracks in Aldershot. We were doing four sessions a day:

5.30am	Session one – Endurance running
7.00am	Breakfast
8.00am	Session two – Football

10.30am	Break
11.30am	Session three – Swimming pool/assault course
1.00pm	Lunch
2.00pm	Session four – Weights
4.00pm	Rest (much-needed)

On the first afternoon, I was doing weighted forward lunges when I felt a twinge in my lower stomach. I sat out the rest of the session and put some ice on the area where I'd felt the pain. Overnight it seemed to calm down and on the morning run it felt ok. But when we started the football, I tried to explode into a sprint and it felt like someone had plunged a knife into me. For the remainder of our time in the army camp, I was pretty limited in what I could do in terms of training. I wasn't the only one.

By the end of our intense week, of the 25 players (including a generous smattering of trialists) that made the trip, 12 were in the treatment room. While we were waiting in a queue for ultrasound treatment with the physio, all of us crammed in a tiny room, 'Knives Out' by Radiohead came on Radio 1. Even as a big Radiohead fan who would always argue with colleagues that dismissed their music as dull and depressing, I had to admit that its maudlin meandering seemed like an invitation to form a mass suicide pact in the circumstances: everyone unsure of the extent of their injury, of their place in the squad and of – ultimately – their job prospects.

We did have a night out to alleviate the impending sense of doom, though. It was pretty standard other than the sight of our Gallic goalkeeper Lionel Perez performing a star turn at a karaoke bar, with women swooning at his feet during his not always wholly intelligible versions of 'Father and Son' and 'Sex Bomb'.

The change in Lionel since the end of the previous season had been marked. Brought in from Newcastle by Roy at great expense after a dazzling performance against us on loan at Scunthorpe, he'd always been pretty quiet and largely kept himself to himself in his first year at the club. I think Becky's arrival and the loss of the comfort zone provided by Roy's faith in him sparked the change. He liked his life in Cambridge and didn't want it taken away. Suddenly he was very vocal in the changing room and on the training pitch, making points and cracking jokes. His karaoke display confirmed his new persona. It was fascinating to see – perceiving a threat to his professional life and personal happiness, he adopted a new approach.

And it worked. He and John had rowed a couple of times in the changing room before, mainly because Lionel's kicking was pretty unreliable and could not consistently hit the areas John deemed so vital. But once he became a bigger influence in the dressing room, his place did not seem under threat at all.

We drove back from the barracks on Saturday, straight to our first pre-season friendly at Cambridge City. With all the walking wounded, we only had 13 players fit to play, but we scraped an unconvincing 1-0 win. Back in Cambridge, I visited a specialist who told me, to my relief, that I did not have a hernia. I had torn a deep core muscle in my abdomen and needed to be very careful for a few weeks. That wrote off my entire pre-season and the first game of the new campaign at home to Brighton.

I eased my way back into training, where our fitness sessions had become quite bizarre. Having enlisted a fitness consultancy firm to help oversee our training, I would watch as Shane appeared to trample all over the young coach Tim's sessions, undermining everything, declaring that players were not pushing themselves and not being pushed hard enough. At one point, David Greene – the centre-half inexplicably signed from Cardiff with an existing knee problem that was never going to heal – was understandably lagging at the back, but his heart monitor showed that he was pushing himself to the limit. Not enough evidence for Mr Westley, who proceeded to trot alongside Greeney for the rest of the run, cajoling him and demanding more effort. Greeney stopped running, and pretty soon he retired from the game. Tim kept trying for a few weeks, but was rendered utterly redundant by the constant questioning of his methods.

Not that I had any problem with a higher focus on fitness in our training. If there was one area of Roy's reign that could have been improved, it was the sports science and fitness side of things. When we had stepped up to Division Two after promotion, on five or six occasions before Christmas we seemed to compete really well for 65-70 minutes before tiring later on, conceding goals and losing points. Although, as the season wore on, we changed from 4-3-3 to a more defensively solid 4-4-2 system, finding some rhythm and pulling off an unlikely escape from relegation, I still thought improving our fitness would help us.

But as I got nearer to full training, after about a month out with the stomach problem, I was more worried about my own fitness than the squad's. Something wasn't quite right, and it was nothing to do with the injury. I just felt sluggish. It always takes a little bit of time to shake the ring-rustiness after a few weeks out, but this was different. I was getting beaten on endurance runs by team-mates who would have been a lap behind me previously. It was as if the extra weight I was carrying from bulking up was in the form of balls chained to my ankles. And I certainly didn't feel any quicker to compensate. If anything the opposite seemed true. I felt less sprightly, less light on my feet.

Nevertheless, it was time to get back out on the pitch. Second-tier high-flyers West Brom at home in the League Cup, live on the doomed ITV Sport channel. I came on at half-time and had a real impact, eventually playing a key role in our late equaliser, before scoring (somewhat fortunately) in a penalty shoot-out that ended in defeat. After one further positive contribution from the bench, John couldn't really leave me out of the first 11. And largely, that was where I stayed for the next three months, plugging away in wide roles on either flank (with a very occasional foray up front), but never feeling very comfortable in what I was being asked to do.

I felt Becky respected my work ethic and saw that I could read balls into the box well – which did lead to three (very similar) goals from long throws – and that kept me in the team even though I struggled with the stipulation that in wide areas you always had to take the ball down the outside of the defender. And I mean always.

Back in the early days of John's reign, our West Ham loanee Omer Riza was substituted within seconds of cutting inside and coming close with a curling effort. Speculative shots, you see, if they do not find their way to the back of the net, almost always end an attack and give the ball back to the opposition, either in the goalkeeper's hands or via a goal-kick. And that, to John, was criminal.

The buzzword of our attacking plan was 'continuation'. Going on the outside meant that, even if you did not manage to get a cross in, you would probably win a throw-in or a corner. Continuation. The more continuations, the more opportunities to get the ball into the box – "never refuse a cross" was another mantra – and the more chances to get efforts on goal. Less ambitious efforts. Ones more likely to find the net.

But I just felt a bit neutered in the wide area, asked to stay wide and only attempt to go one way. Most of my joy since breaking into the team had been when drifting inside from wide positions and joining the strikers. Again it came down to wanting that element of unpredictability in order to beat a defender or find a position where I could cause damage. Having to go on the outside robbed me of that and, not endowed with much foot speed over the first five yards, I found it difficult to consistently manufacture that all-important half a yard to deliver a cross. At times I desperately wanted to chop back onto my left foot, to keep the defender guessing, but I feared being dragged off if my attempt was blocked and led to a break for our opponents. That fear conditioned players into following the designated plans. So I continued to go on the outside, but though I no doubt earned us a lot of throw-ins – *continuation* – I didn't feel very effective. I felt a bit lost going out on to the pitch.

And there was no respite from the disillusionment during the week in training. Lots of 11 versus 11, always with seemingly impossible stipulations. One touch only. No passing backwards or sideways. Everything hooked into areas and chased. If the idea was to show us how our rudimentary tactics would overpower the reserves, who were allowed to play freely, it didn't work. They would often beat us. It just eroded whatever faith any of us ever had in our way of playing.

For the first time, playing football for a living actually felt like work. It was to be endured rather than enjoyed. I got through it by making more plans for my free time with Chelle and friends, giving myself things to look forward to. More meetings for drinks (non-alcoholic during the week, of course), more gigs, more cinema visits. What most people in regular jobs do, I guess.

Despite the odd high, like beating the behemoths of QPR and Cardiff at the Abbey, the on-pitch disenchantment saw us drop to the bottom of the table. The nadir, on a personal and possibly also a team level, came at Colchester. The nightmare began at lunchtime on Friday when, after training, Becky invited us all down to one of the lounges for a spot of pseudo-meditation. While we closed our eyes, John uttered phrases like "we are too strong for them" and "Colchester play tippy-tappy football" like some self-help guru trying to impart assertive thoughts while you sleep. In my head I was just imagining how their tippy-tappy football would rip right through us.

While Colchester were no world-beaters, they had some good players, like the ex-Ipswich veterans Mick Stockwell and Gavin Johnson, French playmaker Thomas Pinault and the prolific former Cambridge frontman Scott McGleish. And their poky, grimy little ground at Layer Road, which made even the pretty poky Abbey seem palatial, had not been kind to me on my last two visits. Things didn't get any better this time.

Despite an Armand Oné solo effort giving us an early lead, we were pegged back for long spells until a quickfire double from McGleish and Johnson ensured we were behind at the break. In the second half we remained on the back foot but, from a rare attack, Armand glided past a few defenders before laying the ball on a plate for me eight yards out, with the goalkeeper stranded beyond the near post. Somehow I contrived to get underneath the rolling ball, scooping it over the bar and into our baying supporters. Scotty finished us off with a third goal and we sloped off miserably to the cramped changing room.

Then arrived the only time that I witnessed Becky's legendary rage (half-time fights with Steve Claridge etc) in the dressing room. He slammed the door and started screaming in his squeaky voice ... "No bollocks" ... "Bullied by a bunch of fannies". A few of the lads got covered in sandwiches scattered from the post-match platter provided by our hosts.

Maybe it was the failure of our Friday psychology lesson that tipped John over the edge. After another winless month, he came in after a 2-0 home defeat to Wrexham – during which the crowd had started a 'Beck Out' chant after just two minutes – and said that he was stepping down, as the fans' campaign against him was "hurting us on the pitch". I immediately felt a huge sense of relief, almost as much as when I realised I'd escaped injury when coming off the scooter a few months earlier.

Much as I loathed playing under John, though, I had sympathy for him as I felt he was compromised from the very start. Any manager brought into a club should be free to mould the team as he sees fit. His job is to win football matches. And regardless of what I or anybody else thought of his methods, John had a pretty good track record of winning football matches, particularly at Cambridge.

But because there was a significant amount of opposition to his return among the supporters, the club quickly seemed to be trying to justify their decision with comments in the wake of his appointment. The noises were all about how John had changed, how the days of visiting teams suffering cold dressing rooms and waterlogged warm-up balls were gone, how there would be no growing the grass long in the corners of the pitch this time around. And this pandering to the disgruntled masses set a landscape in which John's natural instincts would have to be curbed, or at least appear to be. And that seemed to extend to the playing staff.

Lots of the players most popular with supporters were far from perfect fits for a John Beck team. Obviously I was one, but not the only one. Our captain Wanny, the darling of the terraces, had been jettisoned from Lincoln City within weeks when John took charge there – he didn't seem to fit the whirling dervish, 'covers every blade of grass' template of a Becky central midfielder. Neither did Ian Ashbee, another fan favourite.

Lionel's kicking wasn't up to scratch. Andy Duncan wasn't John's type. We didn't want to play football that way and were not suited to it.

In an ideal world, I think John would have wanted all of us out of the way and re-populated the squad with players that fitted his mould. But that didn't really happen. It was almost as if mass changes like that could not be made as they would have sent out the wrong message, conflicting with the 'new John Beck' PR drive which was at pains to point out that we would not be a 'long-ball' team.

The result: a manager with a clear plan but a squad ill-equipped to deliver it. A recipe for disaster.

The overall atmosphere, therefore, was one of confusion. And that confusion inevitably found its way onto the pitch with the players. In that final game against Wrexham, it was almost like I was at war with myself – I still vividly remember winning possession twice in midfield early on and starting to drive forward with the ball, but then, as our training sessions flashed through my mind, I checked and tried to clip the ball over the top for a runner. On both occasions my team-mate ran in a slightly different direction to where I had anticipated, the ball ran through to the Wrexham goalkeeper, and the crowd booed vehemently. Similar internal conflicts were taking place within players all over the pitch. Each mistake or misunderstanding accompanied by howls and growls of disgust from the terraces. The mood in the stadium had grown toxic.

But now the dark days of confusion were finally over. Becky was gone.

League and cup appearances to this point
74 (+30 as sub), 27 goals

10

One Night in Bristol

'Shaggy Is God' had been daubed on a wall opposite the Abbey for as long as I could remember, so it was almost inevitable that the fans' favourite and club record goalscorer would get the chance to succeed Becky, if only in the short term. I was more than happy with that; Shaggy had always been very supportive of me and helpful with extra training drills as I strove to get in, and then stay in, the first team. Popular thinking was that Shaggy – accompanied by assistant Dale Brooks, promoted from youth team manager – would be given a few games to prove himself worthy of the role, while other options were explored. We certainly didn't make it easy for him to make a good impression.

Tranmere away was the first assignment, where Lionel – who despite his obvious Premier League class as a shot-stopper, displayed a frequent tendency for madcap dashes from his line – was red-carded for handling outside the area after only ten minutes. Clint Hill blasted the resulting free-kick into the net, and a Jason Koumas-inspired Rovers took us to the cleaners. 6-1.

The day was notable for me for two reasons: first for ending a ten-game barren spell by converting a late penalty (our first spot-kick since I'd assumed penalty-taking duty) and second for receiving the first booking of my senior career, after almost 100 appearances. It wasn't that I had a particular ambition for a monk-like footballing existence, as if in thrall to my hero Gary Lineker. I just didn't have cause to make too many fouls – at least not the kind likely to merit a caution – and had always thought it was stupid to pick up petulant bookings for dissent or kicking the ball away. Better off staying focused on my game,

I reckoned. I'd always talked to referees, of course, but tried to keep them onside. This time, though, I just snapped.

Tony Scully had been booked in the first half for taking a quick free-kick, but when Koumas did the same to find our top corner and make it 3-0 early in the second half, did we get consistency? Play was not brought back. There was no card. The goal stood. I raced after the referee, who was hastily retreating to the halfway line, to make this point. It's entirely possible that I "approached him in an intimidating manner", as the disciplinary report read. I can still remember feeling the pit of my stomach disappear as I saw Michael Ryan reach into his pocket. Sure, it was only a yellow card, but I still felt pretty embarrassed afterwards.

In Shaggy's second game, we started brilliantly to lead at promotion-chasing Huddersfield, only for another early bath to cost us, this time Stev Angus, ten minutes before the break. As the pressure mounted, Andy Booth headed a late winner. Then came the lowest period of my Cambridge career.

I hated playing under Becky, but I was still in the team. I hated feeling incapable after my inauspicious debut(s), or when I didn't make the bench, under Roy. But I was a kid and there was always the promise of further opportunities to come. However, when we lined up for a practice match in training and I was in what was clearly the reserves, ahead of our LDV Trophy game with Brighton, it really got to me. This was Shaggy. My former team-mate. One of my biggest admirers, or so I thought.

"What's going on?" I asked him back at the ground. "This is your first home game, your first chance to put your stamp on this team in front of the fans. I've put up with all the s*** of the last eight months, and now we finally get the chance to make a new start and I'm not a part of it?"

"We just don't think you're yourself," came the reply. "The extra weight, it's f***** you. Your body's not used to it yet. You don't look sharp. We think you need a bit of a break. When you're ready, you'll get back in."

It probably made a lot of sense. Everyone had been saying it for months. But I couldn't see it. Yes, I'd been less effective this season so far, but I put it down to the team being forced to play in a fashion which negated my strengths. Not that the sluggishness I felt after my pre-season travails had become endemic. What I *could* see was that, with Kits now established and growing into the main centre forward at the club, I was losing the battle to become his partner, to finally nail down the central striker's position I'd always coveted. I was angry.

Over the next eight games, I played occasional, fitful roles – even when Kits missed three games through injury – as I watched the youth team graduates, Dan Chillingworth and Alex Revell, get their chance to impress. Chilli even scored a goal-of-the-season contender, waltzing through top-of-the-table Brentford's defence to net a late winner on Boxing Day. I was happy to see us get three points; we needed every point we could get in what was already looking like an uphill battle to escape relegation. And I wanted to be really pleased for Chilli: a good kid, with plenty of ability, who I'd watched grow up in the youth system alongside my brother, getting to know his dad. But now he was a professional rival, and each time he played well I felt further away from returning to the fold.

A glimmer of hope came in the next game, against Peterborough, when I was partnered with Chilli from the start. But all I did was prove Shaggy's point. I ran around uneventfully for an hour before being put out of my misery. Clearly I wasn't yet ready to be at my best again.

It wasn't like I could suddenly shift the additional weight, there was still hardly an ounce of fat on me. It was my entire build that had changed. Richard Prokas even described me as 'stocky' when comparing me to one of his former team-mates. I laughed (I still think 'stocky' was a bit of a stretch). But I needed to feel comfortable in my physique again, and training hard was the only way to do it.

After I impressed in the ressies against Bournemouth, Shaggy was suitably convinced I was worth another shot. With Kits still injured, I was drafted in against Wycombe on a Tuesday night, three days after a Bobby Zamora hat-trick had downed us 4-3 at Brighton. I made a good start, receiving the ball from a throw-in, eight minutes in, before turning the centre-half and delivering a perfect cross with my left foot for Chilli to head home at the near post. Lionel made another kamikaze bolt from his box and was dismissed early again, but this time we had something to hold on to. We did so quite comfortably, even adding a second through Wanny just after half-time. I played well as a lone striker for the last 35 minutes and was awarded man of the match. It was by no means a vintage display, but it certainly felt like a fresh start.

Maddeningly, I tweaked a groin in the opening stages of our next game, the televised LDV Trophy semi-final first leg against Bristol City. I missed the next two – including, regrettably, what would turn out to be my only ever chance to play at Loftus Road, where the lads played out a 0-0 draw in front of over 18,000 fans – but I retained the confidence provided by the Wycombe performance when I returned to fitness against Colchester at home. I put us ahead with one of the fastest goals seen at the Abbey, after just 16 seconds, which was one of seven I went on to score in the final 18 games of the campaign. But my return to form was unable to spark a turnaround in our fortunes.

In that Colchester game – where another first-half red card, this time for Luke Guttridge, saw us eventually lose 2-1 late on – seven of our outfield players were younger than me, and I was still only 22. As such a young (and small) side, we were just not equipped to succeed in a battle-hardened Division Two, full of big spenders like Cardiff, Reading, QPR, Stoke, Wigan, Huddersfield and Bristol City. But though we were destined to go down, we were at least able to spring one huge surprise and give our suffering supporters something to cheer.

19th February 2002. The best night of my footballing life.

It was a chilly Tuesday night at Ashton Gate, where the second leg of our LDV Trophy semi-final was thought by most to be a foregone conclusion. Bristol City, third in the table and looking for promotion, against us, adrift at the bottom, nine points from safety. City had comprehensively outplayed us in a 3-0 win at the Abbey just before Christmas. With the first leg having finished 0-0, we would have to win away from home to go through, which we hadn't done in the League all season.

Nobody gave us a chance. Certainly not the 12,000-strong, expectant home support. Our hardy band of 250 or so were tucked away in the corner, more in hope than expectation.

But, having made a solid start, on 29 minutes we gave them a bit more reason to believe. Danny Jackman, our Aston Villa loanee on the left wing, spotted me dropping off into space near the halfway line and rolled me the ball. I turned and, with the City defence stepping up in an attempt to catch Armand offside, I ignored the big Frenchman and instead spied Shane Tudor in full flight on the far side. I floated the ball over the back four – all stood still, arms aloft – to put Tudes in on goal. He approached goalkeeper Steve Phillips before unselfishly squaring for Armand, catching up after aborting his over-eager initial run, to slot into the empty net. It was a fine, flowing move from end to end, and silenced the complacent crowd.

Just after half-time, Lionel made a breathtaking stop from Lee Peacock, and on the hour mark we broke again. In similar fashion, I turned from a deep position and this time it was Armand I sent away. His shot was deflected for a corner, from which a scramble ensued and the giant teenager volleyed into the roof of the net. City, stuffing well and truly knocked out of them, tried to exert some pressure, but we were not about to let the lead slip. Brooksie, Shaggy's assistant, had a few sayings up his sleeve, and one of them was, to paraphrase somewhat: "I don't care what it is that motivates you, just make sure it's motivating you today." It seemed particularly relevant here. While most of us were desperate to hold on for the chance to play in a cup final at the Millennium Stadium, Tudes was running round every five minutes reminding the lads about the bonus for getting through. "There's more than a grand each on this," he kept saying. "Come on!"

The full-time whistle eventually arrived. Our ecstatic team – average age a little under 23, excluding 34-year-old Lionel in goal – and backroom staff charged down to the corner to enjoy the moment with our supporters. I say 'moment' – we must have milked it for over half an hour. For me, it was one item of light relief after some pretty unhappy periods over the previous

12 months. Some even in the previous 12 weeks.

The build-up to the final was a lot of fun: getting measured for suits, making public appearances in the city and so on. I was also asked to write about it for the club website, which eventually led to a regular blog (though I wasn't aware of that term at the time) called 'From the dressing room'. I even made a couple of national newspapers thanks to a nice line about HMV customers being more interested in Will Young than Tom Youngs. We went to the stadium the day before, so as not to be overawed on the day. I did radio interviews on the morning of the game at the hotel, and a live TV interview on the pitch before the warm-up. All just a tiny glimpse into the semi-celebrity lifestyle I still hoped to live if I could revive some interest in me from bigger clubs.

The final itself, though, or at least the last half an hour of it, proved to be anti-climactic.

When we got into the dressing room, I wasn't filled with positivity by the team Shaggy had selected. I thought there was a fair bit of sentiment involved. We ended up with three central midfielders all playing in a 4-4-2, which left Luke Guttridge as a slightly uncomfortable wide right. We also had three centre-halves playing, and though Stev had filled in at right back on numerous occasions and defensively was useful to have up against John Hills, one of Blackpool's two effective wingers, when we had the ball he wasn't as accomplished as Warren Goodhind, who'd been playing in the previous few games. Of course I could understand Shaggy wanting to be loyal to a core of players, perhaps those he saw as essential to the future, as cup finals don't come along very often. But purely in footballing terms, I wasn't convinced we were well-balanced.

We were certainly underdogs. Steve McMahon's Blackpool had seen us off 3-0, with ease, at the Abbey only a month previously, and had a very good attack – Richie Wellens prompting in midfield, Martin Bullock on the opposite flank to Hills, John Murphy and Scott Taylor up top. But I fancied that Kits and I could cause a few problems for their centre-half pairing of veteran Ian Marshall – plenty of cunning but lacking in mobility – and youngster Chris Clarke – quick and powerful but prone to a mistake.

The game could hardly have started in worse fashion for us. After only five minutes, one of our lads got left in as everyone pushed out following a corner – which the ITV commentator kindly identified as me, even though I was on the halfway line at the time – and John Murphy, played onside, stooped to head home. But we settled and began to turn the tide after about 20 minutes. Just before the half-hour mark, Ash released me in on goal. As I prepared to edge the ball out of my feet to shoot, I was tripped from behind by left back Tommy Jaszczun. It was a clear denial of a goalscoring opportunity, and had it been a League game, I'm sure Mr Furnandiz would have produced a red card without thinking. But referees don't like to 'spoil' cup finals by adhering to pesky things like the laws of the game, so a yellow card had to suffice, despite my remonstrations. Of more immediate concern, though, was the penalty.

At this point, our record from the spot for the season was scored three, missed seven. I'd missed one recently, which would have given us a late winner against promotion challengers Reading. It made me realise what pressure can do to you when you have time to think about things, rather than having to react instinctively to a ball dropping in the box. I was super-confident going up to take the kick. I'd had a good game, and since being the designated taker, I'd practised at least ten a day after training, barely missing one. Almost always whipped into the left side-netting with my right foot. But with a potentially crucial winner in the offing – as we were entering last-chance saloon territory in our relegation battle – I must have tightened up, sub-consciously. My shot was a good yard or so away from the corner, and Phil Whitehead pushed it round the post.

Now, in Cardiff, it was Wanny stepping up, and he'd missed three out of his four in the campaign. But he belied the pressure to calmly stroke this one down the middle, as Phil Barnes dived left. The Cambridge faithful – making up 9,000 or so of the 20,000 crowd – were in raptures. We were firmly in the ascendancy now; I fizzed a near-post header just over the bar and only a superb last-ditch tackle from Marshall denied me another clear run on goal. Just before the break, I flicked one round the corner to put Kits in for a one-on-one. Sadly, Barnes spread himself well to block, and after Lionel saved smartly from Scott Taylor as the other end, it was half-time. We were well in the game.

Unfortunately, Shaggy had suffered with a severe migraine – he often struggled with them – shortly after we'd gone behind, so hadn't really seen a lot of the last 20 minutes. Clearly all he could remember was our defensive uncertainty in the first 15 minutes. So where I was expecting a positive, 'keep it going'-style team-talk, he basically laid into us and highlighted all the early errors, completely ignoring the fact that, if anything, we were now on top. Afterwards I asked him if he'd been watching a different game and he confessed to being out of it for large parts of the first half. But while I didn't think much of his team talk, I don't think it had any real effect on our performance in the second half. Blackpool – with Marshall's departure through injury probably doing them a favour – upped their game and we couldn't live with them. Clarke scored on the hour, and though we somehow hung in at 2-1 for a while, even nearly equalising when Ash drove narrowly wide, only Lionel kept the score to a semi-respectable 4-1.

I was so disappointed with our second-half display. That we struggled to live with Blackpool's lively attacking play was no surprise, but in possession we couldn't wait to give it back to them. Given the problems Kits and I had caused them before the interval, I was gutted not to get further chances to test their back four. The one time I did, Jaszczun brought me down cynically again, yet still somehow avoided a sending off (we would laugh about it as team-mates at Northampton a couple of years later). The only consolation at the end was the fact that, on a personal level, I'd played pretty well. "Don't let it pass you by," is what most people advise you before a cup final, and I certainly hadn't done that. The Cambridge fans (and oh, what sage judges they are!) voted me the best outfield player, beaten to MoM status only by Lionel's outstanding damage limitation exercise in the last 20 minutes.

Our relegation was confirmed the following weekend, after a 99th-minute equaliser at Oldham denied us a first away win of the season. The last five games were merely early building blocks for the next campaign back in Division Three, but my late run of goals – culminating in a brace at Northampton on the final day – at least saw me overtake Kits to finish as the club's top scorer for the second season running. A crumb of comfort, and a source of hope, at the end of what had mostly been a forlorn and frustrating nine months.

With the Football League joining the Premier League in finishing early due to the May start of the World Cup in Japan, I had a long summer break to clear my head, recharge and be ready for a better season. When we returned, Lionel had moved on – not before becoming the fifth Cambridge player to miss a penalty that season in his farewell home match, breaking the opposing goalkeeper's ankle in the process. Ash had also departed for the division's new moneybags side, Hull. But with the rest of our young squad intact, we were to enjoy a promising pre-season.

League and cup appearances to this point
99 (+35 as sub), 35 goals

11

Small Print, Big Let-Down

Shaggy and Brooksie had developed a new 4-3-3 system for us, with good rotation in midfield and in the forward positions, which bedded in well during the friendlies. There was only one problem for me. With our former loanee Omer Riza arriving on a permanent deal, we now had four players most comfortable in the front three positions.

In pre-season, Omer was not always available (before his deal was settled) and Kits had a couple of injuries, so I was always able to fill either the left-sided or central forward role. And I was playing well. Then, as we entered the final ten days before the season started, everyone became available, so in our final two warm-up games, I was shifted back into the midfield three along with Terry Fleming and Luke. As the two games concerned were against modest opposition in local non-League side Soham and a very callow Tottenham under-21 team, I was able to play freely from the deeper position and break forward at will to arrive where I wanted to be, linking with the forwards and bursting into the box. But with the League campaign about to start, I had serious reservations about my new role.

In my head there were two major obstacles to playing in a more orthodox central midfield role. Firstly, I feared that in a division where many teams tended to bypass midfield, I would end up spending a lot of time on defensive duties, nearer my own goal than the opposition's. And I fancied that there were other players better suited to the defensive side than me.

Secondly, and perhaps more importantly, I thought the role ideally required a greater range of passing than I possessed, or at least felt comfortable of delivering on a consistent basis. As mentioned before, I'd put in a lot of practice since turning professional with regards to striking the ball over distance. And I'd improved greatly. But there's a big difference between feeling confident enough to drive a pass, unopposed, 50 yards to a team-mate in a passing drill – even under the 'pressure' of the lads waiting to take the piss when you shanked it – and spotting and hitting a cross-field pass in a match situation, where the other players are moving and you're being closed down. In those training drills, there was no need for a specific trajectory, it just had to get there. In a match, you'd probably have to get it high enough to miss players in front of you, but not so high that the pass would lose speed and not get there in time. And not so high that it cleared its intended target and sailed into the stands. It was a whole different level of skill. So I was immediately set against the idea.

I'd always felt comfortable as a forward and I'd been playing well in the front three in pre-season, after finishing the last campaign in good form up front. If I was going to persuade any higher clubs to take a chance on me, I felt it would be as a forward. If they came to watch and saw me struggle in midfield, would they come back again? And in more basic, self-preservation terms, my contract was up at the end of the season. I definitely thought I would get another one as a forward, but if I failed as a midfielder and the lads up top did the business, would I be so sure of a new deal?

So perhaps I wasn't fully settled as we went into the first two League games of the season, at home to Darlington and away to Bury. Two sides that favoured a more direct style. I struggled to get into either game and, particularly against Darlington, spent more time tracking opposing midfield runners – as the ball was served up to their big centre-forward Barry Conlon – than I did running forward to join Kits. I pulled Shaggy aside before training and basically begged him to let me play, as before, as a deep-lying striker rather than as a midfielder. "Defensively you'll still get the extra body in midfield when we're out of possession, but I'll be able to get closer to Kits and do what I do best, not receiving the ball 30 yards from my own goal," I pleaded.

Presumably keen to keep his four biggest goal threats on the pitch together somehow, and perhaps in light of my less-than-great performances in midfield, he and Brooksie reluctantly agreed. At Bournemouth the following Saturday, I was where I wanted to be, and our system looked more like a 4-4-1-1. Or perhaps 4-2-3-1, as it's trendy to be branded these days.

It wasn't necessarily a huge change immediately. Sometimes people get too hung up on formations. Or systems. Or whatever you like to call the way a team is set up. As if the system itself is the key to success. But systems are brought to life by the players within them, and no team's version of the same system works in the same way. Certain ways of playing go in and out of fashion, but any formation can work if it maximises the strengths of a specific team's players.

A lot of the systems in which I played during my career could be described as 4-4-2. But if I was one of the two, I would always drop in to make an extra midfield player when we were defending. Particularly if our opponents had a Pirlo-esque deep-lying playmaker (ok, probably a very low-rent facsimile of Pirlo), who would mop up and recycle possession to build attacks. It wasn't only to stop the opposition playing, either. It may have released one of our midfielders to screen their forwards a bit more closely, but for me it was just as much about finding space to be available when we won the ball back. Centre-halves would lose track of me if I looked like I was 'marking' their colleague in midfield. So was any team I played in strictly 4-4-2? Certainly not in a Manchester United, two out-and-out wingers plus Cole and Yorke way.

Looking back, though, after a career that I would like to have lasted longer, I regret what turned out to be a short-sighted decision to press Shaggy for change. Short-sighted for two reasons.

The one which I should have seen coming was that Omer was not really happy in his wide left position. He was a real threat going forward, but didn't enjoy having to protect the full back behind him, and as a consequence didn't always do the best job. And now we were closer to a 4-4-2, we could always swap me with him if things weren't going well.

In two of the next four games (as early as the 25th minute at Southend) we swapped, and from the League Cup tie with Reading – just two weeks after I had scored twice playing behind Kits against table-topping Rushden – the swap would often be from the start. Unless there was a particularly vulnerable full-back that we could target using Omer's blistering pace. So, far from being the deep-lying striker I craved to be, I was mostly back to being a wide midfielder.

The second reason was probably harder to foresee at the time. But the English game was moving on. Physically. Arsene Wenger's arrival at Arsenal had probably hastened the journey over the past five years, and things would soon accelerate at the top level. Players became athletes. All over the pitch. And it trickled down the divisions, making the lower levels ever more physically competitive. Where Roy McFarland had once joked that I was too slow to play for England, by the end of my career I fear he would have been saying I was too slow to play in Division Three. At least up front. It's no coincidence that in the final two years of my career at Bury, my stand-out games at centre-forward came when up against ageing defenders. Where I could do all the clever link play that people admired but also get on the wrong side of my marker and pull away from him.

The one area you could still most easily hide a lack of pace, though, was in the middle of the park. Pace becomes an illusion from midfield, it's all about timing and anticipation. Had I been less worried about what I lacked as a central midfielder, and less bull-headed about remaining a forward, I might have opened up a new avenue of opportunity.

Goals from midfield are a priceless commodity. And I was better than most at watching play develop and bursting forward from deep at the right time, which is how a lot of my goals from the wing came about. Goals can paper over lots of deficiencies (perceived or real) in a player's game.

Not all central midfield players are superb long-range passers. I would have improved with more exposure to receiving the ball in those deeper positions, but equally keeping things simpler would have been fine if I was getting goals. My reluctance harks back again to the pigeon-holing of footballers in the English system from an early age. Never having played as a central midfielder, I felt so uncomfortable with the concept that I was scared to try something new and fail, especially with a place in the team and contracts to compete for. In the early years of my development, when such experimentation carries no professional risk, that discomfort could have been prevented if I'd been put in those situations more often in a match environment. But that's not a good enough excuse. I should still have embraced it at Cambridge. I was popular with fans and management and would have been given time to acclimatise, if I'd given it a chance.

Defending doesn't have to mean bullying your opposite number. Of course it's great when your team has a big physical presence in midfield, as it gives more the impression of total control in that area, a la Patrick Vieira. Particularly in Division Three I thought I might be dismissed as lightweight. But defending can mean just being disciplined positionally, forcing mistakes with good pressing and making interceptions. I could have done that. And if you can score goals, being the best defensive midfielder doesn't seem so important.

A year later, when I saw Yeovil come up from the Conference, under one of my old mentors Gary Johnson, their midfield should have been enough to make me recognise my folly. A diminutive duo of Gary's son Lee and Darren Way – both five foot six – made me look giant in comparison, and neither had any more pace than me. They dictated the game mostly with short passing (though they both had a good range of passing if required) and never got bullied or overpowered on their way to the League Two title.

While both had been midfielders all their lives (Lee had been with me at the Cambridge centre of excellence, while I played against Darren as he came up through the ranks at Norwich), they showed a different midfield prototype was possible. It would have required a bit of re-education on the training field, but that could have been done. I'd made my bed, though, and now I had to lie in it: I didn't want to be a central midfielder.

Being on the left, with Omer up front, was working pretty well for us, if not always for me. We were climbing the table, scoring in every game, but I was getting a bit of stick from some of the fans. "He's not doing anything," seemed to be the gist of it. But basically what it boiled down to was that most of our dynamic attacking play was going through the sprint kings Omer and Tudes, who were both playing well, helping us to turn defence into attack at high speed. By comparison my role was very much a supporting one, as opposed to being the focal point of our attacks under Roy a couple of years previously. Much of the time I didn't have to do much other than get the ball into Kits and let them get on with it. At times I felt almost as much a spectator as those in the stand. But football's a team game and, as things were going well, I wasn't overly bothered. I only scored three and made five assists in the 20 games I played between the Reading cup tie and Christmas, but I still felt that I was playing reasonably well, and making a valuable contribution. Just not as dazzlingly as the others.

Writing my blog for the club website, I always tried to avoid commenting on any personal attacks on me I might have seen on the fans' forum. Which had picked up pace during this recent spell. But I felt the need to react to one. "He never shows any passion," read the message after an away defeat. "I wish he'd just lose it once, punch someone and get sent off. At least we'd know he cared." Passion is definitely one of the most over-used and misused terms in football. It seems to be the default reason spouted by fans whenever a team comes up short. Not that the team in question didn't use the ball well enough. Or that the other team had better players. Or used their skills better. Or were cleverer tactically. Or better organised. It's always passion that's lacking.

Passion – or maybe desire would be a better term – is, of course, important. You have to want to win, and be willing to work hard in order to do so. But desire, or the lack of it, seems to be defined in very narrow terms a lot of the time. Being a chest-thumping, shout and scream-type when things aren't working might play well to the supporters, but it doesn't actually mean you have any more desire than a less demonstrative team-mate. And neither, certainly, does losing your cool and getting a red card.

I always wanted to win. Badly. And the fact that I could keep control of my emotions – which I would argue is pretty helpful in a match situation, allowing for clear decision-making – didn't make me any less driven to succeed. Like everyone else, I'd make mistakes and be found wanting in some games, but it was certainly never due to not caring enough. Which is basically what I put in my blog that week.

The fan in question, if he didn't make the long trip to Exeter to watch our 2-1 victory, would probably have been delighted by the reports coming through on *Soccer Saturday*. Tom Youngs sent off. In a frantic finale, there were four red cards dished out. One to goalkeeper Kevin Miller for tripping me when clean through; one to the hosts' Glenn Cronin for scything down Tudes; and one each to Tudes and Exeter sub Gareth Sheldon for some pushing and shoving. But on Sky they reported five sendings off. And I was the fifth. Despite the fact that I took the free-kick after the melee had been calmed.

I had no idea until I started getting some strange texts through on the way home. From friends. From my brother. From Mum. All broadly asking the same thing: "What happened?" When it became clear what they meant, I was more than a little confused. But there in the papers the following morning was my name, alongside Tudes. Sent off.

Once I'd dealt with the tenth query from surprised friends or family, I thought I could head them all off. I emailed *Goals On Sunday* to let them know that I had most definitely not been sent off, no matter what the Sky vidiprinter or the *News of the World* had said. Chris Kamara and Rob McCaffrey dutifully relayed my message. "Busy bastard!" said a couple of the lads before training on Monday morning.

Tellingly, my most notable game in the months leading up to Christmas was against Bristol Rovers at home, when Tudes was injured. I don't think I did anything remarkably different to what I had been doing previously. It was just that, with Tudes absent, a lot more play had to come down my side and through me. I scored one and made one. And after a draw with Southend on Boxing Day, we were up to third in the League.

But our next three League games proved pivotal. The first, the long trip to leaders Hartlepool, saw us dominate for 40 minutes but, for once, fail to score (it ended up our first scoreless match, 24 games into the campaign). Then a lucky ricochet from a free-kick on the stroke of half-time left us chasing the game. We tried but toiled and succumbed to two further goals in the last five minutes.

Next up were second-in-the-table Rushden at Nene Park. This time our early domination was even more complete, but our shooting boots deserted us. All four of the front players missed chances or saw shots saved by Billy Turley. And when, as a team, we needed to dig in and ensure that our rare profligacy wouldn't prove decisive, we could not. They scored just before the break, as Hartlepool had. And picked us off on the break in the second half, as Hartlepool had. Only this time it finished 4-1.

Finally came the return fixture with Hartlepool. With Tudes out again, and our small squad creaking under the pressure of a string of cup games in between the League matches, we switched to a 3-5-2 formation. Pretty much the only shape in which we could field the players we had available. Again we pressed and pressed, but wave after wave of pressure yielded nothing but an outstanding performance from Anthony Williams in the Pools goal. Even Kits blazed a very presentable chance over the bar. A 0-0 draw saw us tumble down to 12th in a very cramped top half of the table, albeit with some games in hand on many above us. Our promising season was beginning to unravel.

The cup games had been an enjoyable diversion. Three FA Cup replays culminated in a narrow 3-2 defeat at Millwall in the third round, where we gave the Championship side more than a little fright on their own patch. Another run to the southern area final of the LDV Trophy contained some memorable moments, including golden goals from Luke at Luton and Omer in torrential rain at Brentford, where injury had reduced us to ten men. But the extra matches put a big strain on our limited resources – against Bury we fielded only one player (Wanny) over the age of 25, and ended the match with Kits as an emergency centre-half because Duncs was hobbling and there were no more subs available. A sprightly youngster called David Nugent came on to exploit our fragility.

Tudes's right hamstring was becoming a bit less reliable. Our back four was having to swap and change all the time. We were constantly changing formations according to who we had fit. Amid all the disruption, with the free-flowing football of before Christmas no longer on offer, I hit my strongest spell of the season. With many of our players struggling for form thanks to niggles and strains, I had to step back to the forefront of things, and seven goals in 11 games – from a variety of positions – helped to keep us on the coat-tails of the play-off picture. But then even I started to feel overstretched.

In the second leg of the LDV area final, at home to Bristol City, I cramped up in the second half. It was the first time I'd ever done so in my career. I didn't feel any less fit or conditioned. Clearly our punishing run of nine midweek games in 11 weeks, squeezing in all those cup ties, had taken its toll on me. Much as it's understandable for fans to bemoan talk of fatigue in footballers – "why don't you try a real job and see how you feel then, hey?" and other popular refrains – there is a limit for anyone who's trying to perform consistently in such a physically demanding arena. And it seemed I'd reached mine. The squad rotation now so evident at the top level – particularly in attacking positions – is indicative of the greater understanding in and around the game about the dangers of burnout. Reluctantly, I admitted the cramping to Shaggy, when questioned. I didn't want to lose my place in the side but equally I didn't want to give sub-standard performances or, worse, tear a muscle because I was out of gas.

Rested for four matches, I returned refreshed and enjoyed three decent games as we took seven points from nine to stay four points outside the play-off places, with seven games to play. But that was to be my last involvement in a Cambridge shirt – a 2-1 win over Bournemouth at the Abbey on 25th March

2003. Two days before transfer deadline day.

The process which led to my departure had started a month earlier. Rich called to invite me and Chelle to lunch, as Cambridge had got round to offering me a new contract. Shaggy had told me there was one in the offing but that deals for Stev and Kits had to be tied up first as they were the ones with the clearest interest from other clubs. Fair enough. I had to accept I wasn't quite the hot property of a couple of years previously – on the latest *Championship Manager* game, my stats has been downgraded to ones more becoming of a good lower-League player (damn them and their realism!). But after the meal, back at Rich's home office, I was pleasantly surprised. At least initially.

On the table was a fax detailing a two-year extension with a decent rise in my weekly wage, more than I expected the club would be able to afford. I was happy. The only strange thing was a bit of small print near the bottom of the page. It read: "The new terms will be effective from the 1st July." That was a bit odd. It was February. I'd never been offered a new contract before where the new deal didn't take effect for over four months. Rich was equally puzzled, but thought once he'd raised the issue with the club, it would quickly be amended. But it wasn't. The club dug in their heels, and Shaggy confirmed to me, when I raised it with him, that the board were not inclined to make any changes.

I was flabbergasted. I was trying to save up to buy a house for the first time, and the extra thousand pounds or so, if the new money started straight away, would have come in very handy for me. And meant next to nothing to the club. When I thought of all the money they'd splashed on wages over the previous couple of years, on some of Becky's recruits who had made little contribution to the club, I couldn't believe that they would play hardball with me – a dedicated servant who'd been a part of the club for 13 years – for such a paltry amount. It seemed like they didn't really want me to sign.

If that small print had not been present on the contract offer, I would have signed it without hesitation. No matter that I knew there may be better offers out there, both in terms of finance (undoubtedly) and status. I'd had a largely wonderful six years at the Abbey and I loved it at the club.

The fans were brilliant. When I say to anyone that the Cambridge fans are the best I've seen in football, they seem to think: "Well, you would say that. You did well there and fans will always treat you kindly if you do well for them." But it was not just that they sang about me. They sang about *everybody*. Ian Ashbee wore a magic hat. We walked in a Butler wonderland. There was only one Dave Kitson. It wasn't just the more established players, either. Before every game, they would cycle through the lads, singing a song about all of them. Even players who'd just turned up on loan, and would only end up playing a game or two.

We signed Tom Cowan on loan from Burnley via fax one day and the players hadn't even met him until we arrived at Gigg Lane to face Bury. In the warm-up, the supporters obviously didn't have a clue who he was, but they still improvised. "We love you new bloke, we do ..." they chorused. At Northampton, Orient and Bury, I barely heard names sung at all. Certainly not often. Not even the fans' favourite players. It doesn't make them bad fans. They were just as dedicated. But I know that the pre-match welcome at the Abbey really helped players feel at home. And appreciated. Didn't make us better players, of course, but certainly helped with confidence. Which I think is a pretty good aim for people trying to support a team.

But despite the fans, and the fact that we still had an outside chance of making the play-offs, the club's reticence left me annoyed and basically forced me to consider my options. I didn't see the benefit in signing a contract in February that didn't start until July. Why not wait until then to sign it?

I let the club know my position, and as a couple of weeks went by they started to get itchy. They weren't happy for me to wait. By this time, Rich had put some feelers out, if for nothing else than to try to force Cambridge's hand. There had been some tentative interest from Stoke, but nothing concrete. Notts County still seemed keen. But the strongest approach came from our near-neighbours Northampton. We'd knocked them out of two cup competitions and they were languishing near the bottom of Division Two, having had three managers in a matter of months. It would be fair to say I wasn't immediately enthused.

But out of the current turmoil at Sixfields, a new dawn was supposedly on the horizon; a new chairman with grand plans for the future. On hearing that, it didn't seem anywhere near as underwhelming. And if The Cobblers seemed to have potential for growth (even if they looked sure to come down to the fourth tier in the short-term), at Cambridge it was the opposite. Omer was not going to be offered a new deal. Kits had signed his but I didn't expect he would be around for much longer. Tudes was still struggling with his hammy (tearing it in most spectacular fashion by rifling in a 20-yarder against Rochdale).

The squad would only get younger and younger, and we were already regularly fielding sides with an average age of under 23 (perhaps a tipping point where the benefits of youth no longer compensate for the accompanying lack of experience). The longer the club refused to bring forward the start of my new contract, the more time I had to contemplate the likely future at the Abbey. And it wasn't pretty.

That was the main reason for my eventual decision to leave. I could foresee a brighter future at Northampton. And one of struggle at Cambridge. The fact that Northampton could offer, at £60,000 a year, nearly double the deal on offer at Cambridge was, of course, a factor. Chelle and I were still trying to get on the housing ladder. But money, honestly, was not at the root of it. When I say I would have signed without hesitation were it not for the small print shenanigans, I mean it. I would not have asked or expected Rich to contact anyone else.

He came up to Cambridge to meet me after training on deadline day. Northampton's initial offer of £10,000 had been rejected, with United demanding £100,000. But Shaggy was sure they would soon meet somewhere in the middle. I was a bit surprised at Cambridge's certainty that I should leave now rather than run my contract down. As I was under 24, they would have been due a fee when I moved, whether or not they could agree one with the other club. And while it was suggested that they didn't want to risk getting screwed at a tribunal, I thought that was unlikely. A year earlier, Northampton (ironically enough) had been forced, surprisingly, to pay £45,000 to Scarborough for striker Darryn Stamp, even though the Conference club could claim little by way of development. They'd only signed him ten months earlier from Scunthorpe, where he came through the ranks. And he'd only played about 50 games in the Football League.

I thought, if anything, it was me that should have been keener for a move to go through, as in the summer that risk of a tribunal could have been a millstone around my neck, with any suitors comparing me to all the genuine free transfers out of contract. As I'd been with Cambridge since the age of ten, they would have had every claim possible on my development, and I'd played a lot of League games for a 23 year old. Therefore being out of contract wouldn't necessarily have been my golden ticket, so a guaranteed move now seemed sensible.

Just as Rich and I were about to say our goodbyes and jump in the car to Northampton, Shaggy got a phone call. "There's another hat in the ring," he said. Another of our local rivals, Colchester, had come in. While I had mostly miserable memories of Layer Road, I really liked their new manager, the former Reading captain Phil Parkinson. And while Northampton looked likely to be relegated, Colchester were safe in the league above, meaning I would definitely be back in Division Two. But, in the wake of the ITV Digital fiasco, there wasn't much cash sloshing around the Football League. And Colchester could only offer a player exchange. Shaggy didn't fancy the big ex-Norwich striker Adi Coote. So it was off to Northampton.

Their manager Martin Wilkinson gave me a bear hug on arrival and said he was still working on a deal to bring in Bolton striker Delroy Facey to play alongside me up front. Colchester's late approach gave Rich the perfect opportunity to confirm my desire to join The Cobblers, telling Martin (completely dishonestly, of course) that I'd turned down another offer. Contract signed, obligatory photo in new shirt with scarf taken, it was time to go home and see my name in the Teletext deadline day deal list. Eventually reported as £50,000 (though I think strictly it was £45,000 plus a 20% sell-on agreement), it was the third biggest deal, after Herman Hreiðarsson (Brentford to Ipswich, £900,000) and Ben Burgess (Stockport to Hull, £100,000). Time for bed, ahead of a new chapter in my career.

League and cup appearances to this point
143 (+39 as sub), 48 goals

Starting point: The Tottenham shirt that signalled the sudden awakening of my love for football at Christmas, 1986

First steps: One of my early outings for Mildenhall Town under-nines. Nice Panther (not Puma!) boots from Woolworths

VICTORIOUS . . . Mildenhall U-11s team who beat Lakenheath U-11s 0-2 in the Thetford and District League Cu replay semi-final on Sunday.

Youngs goal seals replay win

Read all about it: My first headline in the Newmarket Journal in 1989
© *Newmarket Journal*

Hitting the continent: The Aros Cup in Sweden provided my first taste of European football at the age of 12. That's FA director of elite development Dan Ashworth (top left) and his brother Paul (top right)

On the books: Signing schoolboy forms on a windy night at the Abbey with Paul Ashworth, 1994

Star striker or mascot? It may be hard to believe but I – second from left sitting down – was actually the oldest player in this Cambridge United under-15 team

Turning pro: Mum and brother Andrew sit with me as I sign my first professional contract, watched by Cambridge boss Roy McFarland, youth team manager David Batch and youth development officer Ricky Martin

Breakthrough at last: Pouncing on Roy Carroll's fumble to score a last-minute equaliser against Wigan, earning my first extended run of games in the Football League
© *Cambridge News*

The Full Monty: John Hansen joins me and my pigeon chest in stripping off to pose for a charity calendar
© *Cambridge Fans United*

Abbey days: Joyous celebrations on and off the pitch after an equaliser against Luton. Maybe the fans had a point when they chanted 'Tommy, cut your hair', though
© *Cambridge News*

Final fall: Being brought down for a penalty in the LDV Trophy Final at the Millennium Stadium, 2002. As a team we suffered a similar collapse in the second half
© *Cambridge News*

Happy birthday to me: Celebrating turning 23 with a cheeky nutmeg from a tight angle against Rushden's Billy Turley, 2002. Always a relief to get off the mark for the season
© *Cambridge News*

A new beginning? Four goals in six games against Northampton persuaded
them to seal my signature on transfer deadline day, 2003
© *Pete Norton*

Nice clobber, Cobbler: Don't I look fetching
dressed up for Northampton's Seventies-
themed Christmas party, 2004? Shame it was
a more memorable contribution than I ever
made on the pitch at Sixfields
© *Pete Norton*

Pretty boy: This contorted face while
celebrating my debut goal for Orient
– 23 months after my previous strike,
for Cambridge – earned me the
nickname Dowie at Brisbane Road
© *Leyton Orient FC*

Another long time coming: Getting off the mark for Bury in the local derby at Rochdale. Just a 13-month wait between goals this time
© *Martin Ogden*

Safety assured: Sliding home the goal that settled a lot of Bury nerves on the final day of the 2005/06 season at Notts County
© *Martin Ogden*

They all count: Anthony Gerrard's clearance ricochets off my head and into the net for an unlikely winner at Walsall. Bury are staying up, again (phew!)
© *Martin Ogden*

First class: Graduating at Staffordshire University from the PFA's sports writing and broadcasting degree course. Had to try a few mortar boards before we found one large enough!
© *Staffordshire University*

The dark side: After my 14 years as a player were brought to a swift end, it was time to join the management staff at Mildenhall – complete with initials on my training kit!
© *Cambridge News*

Team photo: My wonderful family – Chelle, Hannah and Orla

12

The Drugs Don't Work

With an hour-and-a-half trip to make to Northampton, I left extremely early for my first day to make sure I wasn't late. Particularly as most of the journey was on the notoriously accident-heavy A14. Just before 8.30am, therefore, I was sat in the petrol station opposite Sixfields, nervously flicking through a newspaper, with 25 minutes until I thought there might be someone at the club to meet me. I hadn't felt butterflies like this since the day I was asked to start changing in the first-team dressing room at Cambridge. That was almost six years before.

Coach Mark Kearney greeted me and ferried me over to the training ground at Moulton College. The session there was taken by Kearney and Paul Curtis, both recently promoted from youth team duties to assist Martin ('Wilko'), himself shifted from the chief scout's role following the abrupt departure of previous boss Terry Fenwick after only seven weeks in charge. That the club was in the midst of a takeover was painfully apparent. On my first payday there was no bank transfer; we were handed cheques, with all the lads advising me to get mine down to the bank as soon as possible to make sure it didn't bounce.

I had to keep reminding myself that this was a move with an eye on the future, not the present. Otherwise I was in real danger of pondering: "What have I done?" A host of players seemed less than interested, knowing that their contracts were running down and would not be renewed. That first session lacked quality and intensity. The squad didn't look particularly capable of mounting the impressive run needed to drag us out of the mire.

Afterwards, I was taken back to the ground to collect my club tracksuit and shown round by 18-year-old striker Steve

Morison, about to make his first League start at Brentford the following day. Slipping past the manager's office, we couldn't fail to hear the hubbub as veteran striker Marco Gabbiadini started shouting at Wilko. It was the very first time in Marco's 18-year career – including over 250 goals and two transfer fees in excess of £1 million (back when that was still a lot of money) – that he had been left out of a matchday squad, not even asked to travel with the team. Stevie certainly had some big boots (and shorts!) to fill.

From training, not that we did much, it was clear that I would play on the left wing. Against our mid-table hosts, we held our own in the first half but conceded shortly after the break, and another couple late on finished us off. My debut had been so-so; Morison and strike partner Lawrie Dudfield were better at stretching the defence than providing a target for me to play into and follow, so most of my possession was out on the wing, somewhat isolated, where Bees right-back Michael Dobson was a formidable opponent. I'd heard in training a couple of times the coaches say "leave him alone, give him room" to the strikers about me, the kind of thing you'd normally say when you don't want them to fill the space in front of a flying winger. Precisely the opposite of what I wanted from them. It got me wondering whether the staff had ever actually seen me play. As we built up a bit of a head of steam before Brentford's second goal, I had one half-chance, latching on to a loose ball and firing against the outside of the post from a tight angle. It wasn't a dream debut, by any means.

The following Friday, for my home bow, champions-elect Wigan were in town. We were no match for them, but I did have the chance to announce my Sixfields arrival with a bang, midway through the second half. Playing a sweet one-two with Gabbers (restored to the squad this time) I burst through to just beat Latics goalkeeper John Filan to the ball. But at the last minute I opted against lifting the ball over him, preferring to sell a dummy and try to round him. Bad move. He read my intentions and managed to fingertip the ball off my toe. A goal might have given us a chance or – more likely – just caused

Wigan to re-assert themselves, but either way it would have been ideal to get off the mark in my first home game. And stop the guy sitting next to Mum shouting: "50 grand for that?!" in her ear.

During the next week in training, a new assistant manager was appointed under Wilko. It was Richard Hill, who I remembered as Northampton's midfield scoring sensation from my first subscription to *Shoot!* magazine many years previously. The dyed-blonde mullet I recalled had long since bitten the dust, though, replaced by a bouncer-like skinhead look. By this stage, it was clear that Wilko was not really a manager by any criteria that I recognised. A self-confessed 'non-coach', he wasn't always at training, and, when he was, he mainly made what I thought were very 'non-coach'-like comments, which often left the lads a bit puzzled. He was a nice enough guy, who'd clearly developed a good reputation and been trusted as a chief scout. But a manager? I wasn't so sure.

The next two games ushered us firmly towards the trapdoor. At Port Vale, we came back from a goal down to grab what looked like an 89th-minute winner. Deployed up front with Gabbers, I had a good second half. A hand in the first goal, an assist for the second, with only a fine save stopping my fierce drive in between. But in a mad stoppage time period, we contrived to concede twice and throw away all three points.

Next up were fellow strugglers Stockport at Sixfields, who blew us away with a three-goal salvo in the first 24 minutes. Summing up our disarray was substitute Richard Hope being called to come on soon after the third goal, but not having his boots with him on the bench. Paired with Gabbers again, I had another chance to break my Cobblers duck after we linked up once more, but Ola Tidman got down to block. At least I was getting the opportunities, I kept telling myself. Even in a doomed team. That could only be a positive, moving forward.

But that optimistic view of the future survived for around 90 seconds of our next game at Tranmere. I evaded big centre-half Ian Sharps, but then, as I prepared to shoot, got crunched by recovering left-back Shane Nicholson. My right ankle crumpled and, with some assistance, I hobbled off.

As the lads made their way out for the second half, I was briefly left in the dressing room alone with Hilly, who gave me some uncharacteristically warm words of encouragement before heading back to the bench. "You'll be alright with me," he said. "You can play." I'd enjoyed Hilly's training sessions, few that there had been. He'd given me some valuable advice about holding a more central forward position for longer, not drifting outside the line of the 18-yard box as play developed. Otherwise I was eating up some of the angle which allowed me to drop into space between defence and midfield, which he'd seen I was good at in the game at Port Vale. I hadn't even noticed my inadvertent wandering. That's the kind of thing good coaching can do. But I was to enjoy precious few further pearls of Hilly's wisdom in what turned out to be a torturous next nine months (of which he was only around for four and a half).

On crutches for the next week – I nearly fell down some stairs while house-hunting – the ligament damage kept me out of the last two games and ensured I would have to traipse in the 77 miles from home for another four weeks of treatment and rehab after the season had ended. In my little green Ford Fiesta. Which somehow got me a spot in *Nuts!* magazine as part of a feature called 'Footballers Who Drive Sheds' – a sidebar to a piece on stars and their Aston Martins and Lamborghinis. Others included were Wayne Rooney, Robert Pires, Ashley Cole and Zinedine Zidane. Quite how I came to join the party I don't know. All of their 'sheds' must have been cast aside years ago; I was still driving mine.

Eventually I got the all clear from physio, Den Casey, after a fitness test, meaning I could finally start my summer break. It was a pretty hectic one: Chelle and I buying and decorating our first house (which, thanks to the bumper new contract, was a 4-bed detached in Duston, a village on the edge of town) before getting engaged and starting to plan a wedding for the following summer.

But the real hive of activity was Sixfields, where the long-mooted takeover finally went through, as promised when I signed. In came the Cardoza family as owners with big ideas, quoting feasibility studies which put Northampton alongside Brighton as potential 'sleeping giants' due to the vast catchment areas of both clubs. Wilko was handed a weighty war-chest to secure promotion back to Division Two, and set about spending it in attention-grabbing fashion. After Paul Reid and Duds made their loan moves permanent, a further ten new faces flooded through the door, including the club record £165,000 signing of winger Josh Low from Oldham. I knew I had to hit the ground running on our return for pre-season training to avoid becoming the forgotten man of the club's frenzied recent transfer dealings. But maybe I hit the ground a bit too hard.

As ever, I wanted to take a free chance to impress on any distance running, and only Paul 'The Machine' Trollope and youth team graduate Aaran Cavill got the better of me. Our early pre-season schedule was archaic, though. I'd come from Cambridge, where the last pre-season was very scientific, devised by the physio Stuart, with more ball-work than out-and-out running. It was still as hard as any I'd experienced. At Northampton it was long run after long run. Around a town centre park one day, around a nearby fishing lake (on unforgiving concrete) the next. Laps and laps of the track around the back of the stadium for one session, laps and laps of a local woodland area (complete with solid ground and large tree roots jutting out) for another.

After four days, my right knee was really struggling. The next day, as we got on to the grass – in boots – for the first time, I tried to battle through. But my limp got more and more pronounced as the session went on. We were due to leave for the United States 24 hours later, and Wilko wanted me there, injury or not. "It'll be good to get you in with all the new lads," he reasoned. "We're there for 12 days, you'll probably be able to train a bit towards the end." But I didn't think I would. And so it proved.

It was a pretty lonely 12 days. I travelled with the lads to training each day but could only do sit-ups and other strengthening exercises on the sidelines. Even just jogging, it felt like razor blades had been inserted into the outside of my knee. Most of my training was done on my own in the pool at the hotel. That Chelle was at home alone, nearly 4,000 miles away, in a new house with no friends or family nearby, made it all the worse. Though I finally got some company when new signing Ashley Westwood ('Westy') injured his knee messing about on a golf buggy, I was so glad to get back to England.

Being injured is always horrible. It's an occupational hazard for a footballer, of course, but doesn't get any less frustrating the more times you go through it. That frustration was exacerbated here by being injured at a new club where I was not established, where no-one knew me, what I was like as a person, or as a professional. The experienced Den had accurately diagnosed my problem straight away: bursitis, or "runner's knee". But I think the fact that an MRI scan confirmed there was no ligament damage, and that bursitis is seen as a minor issue which normally clears up on its own, coloured everyone's opinion that I would be fine in a week or two with some rest. At Cambridge, with people who knew me well, if I'd said I was in severe pain, it would have been taken seriously. They knew I rarely missed training. And that I was perfectly happy to play through a bit of pain if at all possible. At Northampton, they didn't know those things. And I don't think my pain was taken very seriously. I felt that I was being looked upon as soft. But I'd never experienced such acute pain.

After a couple of weeks' rest didn't clear things up, I was sent for a cortisone injection. It was designed to take away the inflammation and allow my knee to get back to its normal state. A few days later, I was able to start running, pain-free. I was so relieved.

Having missed most of pre-season, I was some way short of match fitness, but with a week's training under my belt, I was drafted back onto the bench for our home match with Darlington. I was on the bench a further three times, unused each time (although Wilko did try to send me out to warm up late on at Cheltenham before I informed him that we'd already used three subs). But then I started to feel the pain again, in training. "Well, it worked to start with..." appeared to be the logic in sending me back for another injection. I was a bit worried, having heard horror stories about cortisone-hidden injuries from the Seventies, but I was prepared to go with Den and the doctor. Same outcome.

Initially, I felt fine. Back on the bench for Carlisle at home, where this time I was able to come on and have an impact in a 20-minute burst on the right wing, playing a part in our second goal. After scoring in a ressie match against local side Bugbrooke the following evening, I was looking forward to training on the Thursday.

We were on the pitch at Sixfields, and Wilko got us into a huddle. "Right lads," he began. "This is going to sound daft, but God came to me in a dream last night and told me the team I needed to play." More bizarre (if that's possible) than his introduction was his insistence that I was going to play in central midfield, in a 4-4-2 formation, alongside Troll. Even more so than at Cambridge in the 4-3-3 system, I was initially bemused at the idea. Especially as I'd come on as a wideman and done well on the Tuesday. Chris Hargreaves, the central midfielder and fans' favourite, was equally uncomfortable with being stationed wide on the left. The discomfort must have shown in our attempts to make things work in the session, as after only 15 minutes or so Wilko called proceedings to a halt, saying we were "making him nervous".

Quite how he expected his divine idea to become fully-formed immediately before his eyes, I'm not sure. In a very unfamiliar role, I might well have been a bit slow to find my feet, but I was fully prepared, however reluctantly, to give it my best shot. Wilko, and therefore presumably God, had other ideas. When we reported for training the next day, not only was Greavsie restored to the central midfield berth, but I was out of the side completely. No wonder I'm an atheist (or maybe that was the problem!).

As it turned out, against Macclesfield on the Saturday, Martin Smith ('Smudge') got injured after 30 minutes, so I got an hour up front. I did ok, holding the ball up well and releasing some decent passes, even getting MoM in the local paper. But I didn't have any real chances. Boaz Myhill played well for the visitors to ensure a 0-0 draw.

The fickleness of football supporters was summed up in the readers' comments page of the paper, where fans could text in their thoughts. On the same page (possibly even from the same contributor), one comment regarding the Carlisle game praised my 'exciting contribution' as a substitute, while another relating to the Macclesfield game concluded that 'without Smith we've got nothing, and Youngs isn't the answer'. The contrasting opinions were just four days apart. Clearly I had some work to do to prove my worth.

I did start in the 5-2 battering at Premier League Portsmouth in the League Cup – where we were down to ten men inside ten minutes – but I was back on the bench for the trip to an in-form Oxford side. We were 3-0 down by half-time, and though there were no further goals after the break, we were comprehensively outplayed throughout. I was given a thankless half-hour on the left as we tried to limit the damage, and somehow became the focus of Wilko's ire at the end. "I brought you on, and what do you do? You were yards off them," he proclaimed. My lack of respect for him was now complete. If my bit-part appearance was the first thing he could find to criticise in that shambolic performance, where we could have been six down before I even entered the fray, I saw no hope left in the situation. "They're singing 'Wilko out' in the stands, and I feel like joining in," continued the besieged boss. He may as well have done, as he was gone by Monday morning.

Wilko's departure left Hilly in charge. "I'll be honest with you, I'm throwing my hat into the ring," he told the lads. He'd appeared to show his true colours in the dressing room for the first time at Oxford, grabbing shirt collars and squaring up to a few lads. When a couple pushed him away, he came back: "Oh, you want to fight me, do you? Well you didn't want to show any f****** fight out there, did you?" Any admiration I'd had for him as a coach from those early weeks had vanished after the pre-season trip to America. The lads nicknamed him 'Finchy' after the loutish bully from The Office. His two games in charge resulted in a 0-0 draw at Lincoln and 5-1 thumping at home to promotion favourites – a tag we'd held before the season – Hull. "Well, I guess that shows how much you wanted me to take over, doesn't it?" he said afterwards. Quite right.

I don't think it's entirely fair to judge Hilly on his brief period at the club, though. I never felt he ever really saw eye to eye with Wilko. He would probably have made very different selections were he in sole charge, and been able to work up better plans for those revised selections on the training ground, where he was unquestionably a good coach. Players tend not to care whether they actually like a manager as a person if they're organised well and winning.

In between those two matches, I played for the reserves at Peterborough and had to come off at half-time, feeling my knee pain coming on again. Having had some genuine involvement with the first team, however chaotic it had been, I was devastated. More in hope than expectation, I iced the knee all night and tried to join in training the next day. I barely got round a warm-up lap of the pitch before the razor blades were back.

Den was still determined that I should not need an operation, so took me for some analysis in Nottingham. The specialists looked at my gait and the shape of my feet, legs and upper body. Apparently recognising some flaws, I was given some specially-moulded orthotic insoles to correct my foot position while running, and a programme of exercises to strengthen the lower right-hand side of my core and my right thigh muscles.

I was sceptical, to say the least. I couldn't quite fathom how my gait could be responsible for the problem. It wasn't like I'd had some serious injury that had caused my gait to change. I was running the same way I had done all my life. I went through quite serious physical changes during Becky's tenure at Cambridge, but that was over 18 months before and any effect would surely have not been so slow to develop. Whatever had caused the knee to flare up (and I was certainly putting my money on the punishing, old-fashioned pre-season regime playing a part), I didn't think new shoes and muscle-toning would sort it out. But, depressing as it was to be back, day after day, in the dungeon-like gym around the back of Sixfields (where I'd spent over half my time since first stepping through the door at the club), I did my exercises religiously for four weeks to see if it would work. Unsurprisingly, it didn't. I tried to run and nothing had changed.

Still the club weren't keen to operate, so I was sent to a swanky Chelsea hospital to have another cortisone injection, this time with the doctor watching the insides of my knee via an ultrasound scanner, to make sure of getting right to the root of the problem. He could see the bursa was still highly inflamed, but thought that with a bit more precision to the procedure, he could effect a more permanent change. I was told to avoid any impactful exercise for five days to allow the injection to work its magic. After a quick shopping trip down the King's Road, I got the train back to Northampton and patiently waited the advised five days.

Then, down at the training ground we sometimes shared with Northampton Saints rugby club, under the watchful eye of Den, I started to jog around the pitch. There were a few twinges on the opening lap, but I persuaded myself that, having not run for a while, there were bound to be. So I ploughed on, hoping that the pain would not build. It did. By the third lap, I was basically limping. I could have cried. "You're going to have to go under the knife," said Den. John Deehan, part of the new management team that I'd barely seen despite them being in charge for six weeks, wandered over for confirmation of what he could see plainly with his own eyes. I needed an operation.

Former Norwich and Wigan boss Deehan (known as 'Dixie') was assisting Colin Calderwood, plucked from working with the youth team at Tottenham. I was certainly intrigued when he was appointed. It seemed to me like a very exciting move from the club, rather than bringing in a more established name from the managerial merry-go-round. I couldn't wait to see and hear his ideas in training. To have my chance to stake a claim for a place in his team. But I had to wait. A long time.

It was so infuriating watching games go by, each one giving Colin and his staff a further chance to evaluate the players, to decide who they wanted to keep, to identify where the team and squad needed strengthening. Without any input from me whatsoever. He was formulating plans while I was just an ephemeral presence on the sidelines, an afterthought, a 'maybe … if he can get fit'. No matter what he may have heard about me from other sources – and hopefully it was mostly positive – he would need to see it on the pitch before he could factor me into his thinking. And that still seemed a long way off.

League and cup appearances to this point
149 (+43 as sub), 48 goals

13

An Unhappy Reunion

I was booked in for surgery in the second week of December. The well-respected consultant surgeon Bill Ribbans – famed for once being entrusted with fixing Michael Schumacher's leg after a crash at nearby Silverstone – did the procedure at the Three Shires private hospital. It was surreal waking up after what seemed like minutes but seeing the clock on the wall had moved on more than two hours. Professor Ribbans came to see me and showed me the excised bursa, which he said "did look in a bit of a sorry state". The problem had become chronic and no amount of injections – the puncture points of which could clearly be seen on the removed sac – or strengthening of connected muscles was likely to change that.

He cautioned that as there was now nothing between the tendon and bone on the outside of my knee, I may be at risk of accelerated wear and tear issues in the future, but he was pretty confident that I'd not even notice a difference from before the injury. The hospital were keen for me to stay a third day for my recovery, but, luxurious though the hospital was, and much as I'd enjoyed being introduced to the BBC daytime staple, *Homes Under the Hammer*, I was desperate to get home. Chelle drove us back to Duston at a snail's pace, with me strapped awkwardly in the back, keeping my leg extended. Two weeks later, on Christmas Eve, I was back at the hospital to have my stitches removed and the job signed off as satisfactorily complete. I got the green light to put down my crutches. In the meantime, it had been the team who looked in need of some surgery.

I'd braved the Friday night match at home to my old club Cambridge, but after an early red card for Chris Willmott ('Motty') a late goal consigned us to a third defeat in four, leaving us down in 17th, just four points above the relegation places. On Boxing Day, I sat nervously at home watching Sky as we entered the last 15 minutes at Bristol Rovers 1-0 down, a result which would have seen us drop further to 21st, perilously close to the drop zone. But two late goals – including one for Richard Walker, on loan from Villa at a second club to potentially obstruct my first-team ambitions – provided salvation, sparking a run that would eventually deliver 16 wins from 24 and a play-off place.

While it was of course heartening to see my team-mates creeping steadily towards the top half of the table, I still felt completely detached from it all as I worked my way back to fitness. It was hard to share the boys' excitement at drawing Manchester United in the FA Cup when I knew I would not be involved.

Ten days before that encounter came my first match action for four months at Brentford in the ressies. It soon become clear that Mr Ribbans was spot on in saying I'd feel no ill effects from the surgery. It made me wish I'd pushed harder for an op all along. I think that because it wasn't an injury I'd had before, and I didn't really know, therefore, how best to deal with it, I didn't feel comfortable rocking the boat. But with the knee seeming perfectly fine, the previous six months or so now felt like a needless waste of time.

After two further second-string outings, Colin was suitably impressed to name me on the bench for the visit of Rochdale. Coming on at 1-1 with 12 minutes left, I saw us score twice in five minutes to seal the points before the moment I'd been dreaming of for ten-and-a-half months arrived. Well, I thought it had. Derek Asamoah's shot came back off the goalkeeper and I stooped to head in. Finally, my first goal for the club, I thought. A monkey off my back. A new start. I leapt in pure jubilation in front of the home fans. But I turned round to see the referee indicating a free-kick for offside. I must have looked a right plum. I hadn't even checked over at the linesman (sorry, assistant referee) because I'd started my run from next to Derek as he struck the ball. I didn't see how I could have been offside.

I was gutted. But at least I was back on the pitch.

A couple more introductions from the bench, and a couple more near-misses in the quest to break my duck came and went – great save by Sam Russell at Darlington, shot blocked at Scunthorpe – before I was granted an opportunity from the start. Leyton Orient at home was my first Football League start for 313 days. And the last one, at Tranmere, had lasted for two minutes.

I was deployed on the left hand side of the forward line in Colin's innovative 3-4-3 system, and had a lively first half: always on the move, buzzing around and causing defenders to think. But my big chance came after 20 minutes and I blew it. Latching on to a Marc Richards flick on, I was in on goal, but after a good touch to set myself up, my crisp left-foot strike went, agonisingly, inches wide of the far post. Early in the second half we were reduced to ten men and I, understandably tiring, was replaced by Josh Low. A good move, as it happened, as his cross soon drifted into the far corner to give us a somewhat fortuitous victory.

After getting through my first game in months, Dixie and Colin – who said I'd done pretty well, though I knew I'd need to do better – gave me a rest for the Tuesday trip to Kidderminster, in preparation for our next match. At Cambridge. "We're sure you really want to play in that one," said Dixie. I agreed. Could there be a better game and venue to get back on track?

Well, yes, as it turned out.

The day didn't start well. Reporting to Sixfields for brunch ahead of a 1.00 kick-off at the Abbey, I knocked the beans off my plate, covering my white polo shirt. At least it gave the lads a laugh. They were laughing again, on our arrival at the ground, as we walked through to the dressing rooms. All the staff, from secretaries to chefs to groundsmen, gave me a warm welcome. "Bloody hell, it's like a film star returning home!" chuckled a few of my team-mates. Further hilarity ensued in the dressing room when the teamsheets came through. Colin and Dixie were asking me about the attributes of the United players, particularly the physiques of a couple of young lads they were not familiar with. As I gave them my pretty comprehensive lowdown on the opposition, my colleagues were giggling in the background. "Please boss, give me some more," Reidy said, posing as me. "Not just Cambridge players, test me on anyone!" Even though I'd spent much of my time at the club in the treatment room, far away from the lads, my status as a Statto had still broken through.

Offering good advice on the Cambridge line-up proved the highlight of my day. From then on, I didn't handle things at all well. The combination of wanting so much to get my Northampton career properly underway, and also to disappoint the few naysayers in the home crowd, made for a perfect storm of nervous energy. I felt drained and empty after a few minutes. My decision-making was going haywire. My touch was not as sure as normal. Then came the chance to banish those nerves.

About half an hour in, Smudge spotted my astutely-timed run and clipped the ball over the top into my path. With the defence pushing up for offside, I was completely in the clear. All I needed to do was have a good touch out of my feet. But no. As I tried to bring the bouncing ball under my spell, I didn't push it far enough in front or to the side, keeping it somewhat stuck under my feet and leaving me with no angle in my approach to good friend Marshy in goal. As a consequence, I had to slow down, allowing Marshy to narrow the angle, at which point my subconscious started contemplating all the times I'd bared down on him in training, and what he might be expecting me to do. The sloth and indecision borne of that bad touch proved fatal as Dan Gleeson, one of the youngsters I'd been describing in the dressing room beforehand, recovered to toe the ball away for a corner.

I really did want the ground to swallow me up. I think I even held up an apologetic hand to the enraged Cobblers fans behind the goal, such was my embarrassment. I hoped for an opportunity to redeem myself. I tried to keep involving myself in the play as much as possible. But early in the second half my nightmare was complete when I felt my groin twang near the halfway line.

Somehow, despite a second-half onslaught from Cambridge, we clung on and then nicked the three points from a stoppage-time corner when Motty lashed home. After the game I went home to a friend's birthday party in Mildenhall, but didn't really want to speak to anyone. It felt like I might have just blown my best chance to really establish myself at Northampton.

It was only a minor tweak to my groin, typical of the kind often suffered when returning from a lengthy spell out injured. But by the time I was fit again, two weeks later, the gaffer had brought in two strikers to bolster the squad. Eric Sabin, the pacy, elegant Frenchman from Swindon, was to score five goals in our final 11 games of the regular season. Strangely, the other addition was Shaggy, sacked as Cambridge manager shortly after our win at the Abbey. Just like Roy at United, Colin thought Shaggy would be an excellent option to have on the bench. A late equaliser in our home match with Southend proved the gaffer right.

I was restricted to a couple of brief substitute appearances as Colin and Dixie informed me that I looked like I needed a good pre-season. It was hard to argue, but I worried that – as they would already be needing to make firm plans for the future, yet had seen so little of me – I had slipped a long way down the pecking order in their eyes. But I hoped to stay fit on the off chance that an injury crisis or something similar might offer me an opportunity in what was becoming a promotion charge.

It did, to a point. A red card for Eric left open a spot on the bench for the home leg of our play-off semi-final with Mansfield. But within minutes of my introduction, the away side grabbed a 2-0 lead and I never got into the game. In the stand for the second leg at Field Mill, I was as disbelieving as the fans around me when we found ourselves 3-0 up, and in front on aggregate, just after half-time. As it looked like we were on our way to the final, there was a real conflict of emotions in me.

Awful as it would be personally to return to the Millennium Stadium as a spare part, as 17th or 18th man, carried with it would be the chance to become a Division Two player again. I appeared to have a difficult job ahead, trying to prove myself worthy of a place in Colin's team, but it would be better to take on that job in as high a league as possible. And I knew I could cut it in that division, if given a shot. Soon it was all moot, in any case. A couple of controversial refereeing decisions helped Mansfield back on level terms, and we lost on penalties. Division Three again, then.

The customary round of end-of-season meetings took place the following day. Colin and Dixie re-iterated that with a pre-season to regain full fitness, I would have every chance to stake a claim. Dixie, in particular, seemed a bit vexed that I struggled to identify clearly my best position. But I wasn't sure what system they would opt for, given a summer to work on it, so I didn't want to pin myself down.

What I could be clear on, though, was that I would come back super-fit and raring to go. We were all given close-season maintenance programmes to follow, and heart monitors to record our efforts. There was no hiding from the work. I think Westy tried to stick it on his dog once but found the heart-rate readings weren't exactly compatible! I stuck rigidly to my schedule, even pounding the treadmill on my honeymoon in Malta, after Chelle and I were married in June at nearby Whittlebury Park, next door to Silverstone race track. When the squad reported back for pre-season, I felt in tip-top condition. I clearly looked it, too, judging by the comments from the coaching staff.

The heart monitors were used in all sessions so that our new fitness coach, Ryland Morgans – who would graduate from The Cobblers to Fulham, then Swansea, Wales and eventually Liverpool – could track everyone's performance. My only problem with this was my freakishly low heart rate. Until he was able to build up any history of our statistics, Ryland used generic targets for everyone to reach during our runs. But his target of 180 bpm was right at the very top of my range. So while the other lads were hitting it quite easily and then maintaining an even pace to stay at that level, I was charging round, lapping all and sundry and still not reaching it. It wasn't until we returned from a training camp in Seville that Ryland calculated some more reasonable targets for me, based on my true resting rate of 44 bpm and a very top whack of 182 (I did get there eventually, just the once!).

The Seville trip was shambolic to say the least. The training facilities were average and the three opponents lined up for us would have given Sunday League football a bad name. The 15-0 demolition job which rounded things off was embarrassing for all concerned. I lost over half a stone in water during the game. As the feckless opponents couldn't get out of their half (quite literally), there was absolutely no let-up for the forwards. I couldn't sleep that night, my calves were so painfully full of lactic acid.

I roomed with Scott McGleish in Spain, our new arrival from Colchester, for whom he'd scored a hat-trick against us in the LDV Trophy. Scotty was the best finisher from crosses I ever worked with. Headers (an inch shorter than me, he had a prodigious leap), volleys and even overhead kicks, his technique was superb. You couldn't always rely on him to look after the ball in general play, though he always tried his best, but get the ball in the box and he would finish. He scored goals wherever he went, including Sixfields.

His presence didn't fill me with hope for my prospects of playing many games, though. Between us, we didn't offer much pace or physicality. With Marc Richards and Eric offering those qualities, as well as Smudge the schemer, there was plenty of competition for places up front.

So I could certainly have done without my shoulder popping in and out of its socket after a fall in a friendly with Aston Villa's under-21 side. Unavailable for a couple of the pre-season matches, I was set for the bench as the season started at Swansea, with a front three consisting of Smudge tucked in behind Rico and Scott. We won, but Smudge suffered an injury, offering me a glimmer of hope. Though Eric was drafted in, after four not entirely convincing performances from the team, I came on late to good effect against Gillingham, in the League Cup (where I smashed a shot against the bar from 20 yards), and Leyton Orient, earning another go from the start at Scunthorpe, a day before my 25th birthday.

The first half was alright, although Andy Keogh banged in a real bolt from the blue to put us undeservedly behind at the break. On the hour mark came my big moment. A good team move cut through the Scunny backline and left me with just the goalkeeper to beat, ten yards out in the inside left channel. It was the kind of regulation chance you yearn for to end a drought. Alas, I tried to bend it round the goalkeeper into the far corner, but didn't impart enough curl and the ball arrowed narrowly wide of the far post. I was taken off a few minutes later, at which point Chelle – who'd made the trip alone from Northampton as she knew I was playing – sheepishly left the ground, a few choice insults aimed at me still ringing in her ears. I was distraught on the bus home. Another opportunity passed up. I doubted I would get many more.

But a couple of weeks later, a freak double injury blow in training – Scott and Rico dropping on the same day – opened the door again. Darlington away. It was comfortably my best performance in a Northampton shirt (not that there was much competition for that title!). I played in behind a front two of Steve Morison and Eric. Darlington were generous in allowing space between midfield and back four and I exploited it, providing chances for both front men in the opening stages. I could feel my confidence returning with each successful touch of the ball. All that was missing was that elusive goal.

In the first half, a loose ball dropped in my vicinity from a corner and I swivelled to fire in a shot, but Sam Russell (again, like a few months previously) made a brilliant block. Then in the dying seconds, Motty headed the ball back across goal and, with the score 1-1 and a winner beckoning, I got fractionally under the bouncing ball and my effort skimmed the top of the crossbar. Our performance, particularly with a patched-up side, deserved that winner. My performance deserved that winner. But, having got so much right during the game, I got it wrong at the vital moment.

I kept my place for the next three games. Against Southampton in the League Cup I had another great chance to score, but a last-ditch block from Andreas Jakobsson deflected my shot over the bar. In that game it was really hammered home to me just how athletically advanced the Premier League had become. Every time I thought I'd bought myself a bit of time and space, including for the shot, some player was able to eat up the ground and get back at me. I didn't lose the ball constantly, but I just couldn't get away from anyone.

Against Bristol Rovers I had another good day, helping Scotty to win us the game, but Kevin Miller tipped my best effort around the post. Finally, at Yeovil I was withdrawn at half-time after the hosts' Johnson-Way axis in midfield was completely dominant, causing Colin to switch to 4-4-2. The returning Smudge and Eric combined for the latter to provide an equaliser. And that, pretty much, was that for my Cobblers career.

It wasn't for the want of trying. I just couldn't get things going. Everything was in place for a player to show their best at the club. In David Kerslake and future England goalkeeping coach David Watson, the backroom staff were excellent. And the Premier League background of all the management team ensured a top-level set-up. Personalised, measured weight-training and exercise regimes, undertaken together as a squad. Good food after training. Even the hassle of washing and drying your own training kit, at home, was taken away. It was all done at the club by kit man Norman and we picked it up each morning.

The worst thing of all was that I got on well with Colin and I felt he was willing me to succeed. He liked my professional approach – one day at training, cringe-inducing though it was, Dixie called me out in front of everyone as an example of professionalism: "Never forgets his heart monitor, never forgets his water bottle, never forgets to clean his boots, just gets on with things even when he's not in the squad..." Colin also seemed to like the way I thought about and tried to play the game. When he brought me off at Yeovil, he was almost apologetic, saying that without my diligence in dropping in to give an extra man in midfield, we'd have been completely over-run. Another time, I was on the bench and, as the opposition were allowed an easy route to switch play from a deep throw-in, he screamed in frustration: "For f***'s sake, if Tom Youngs isn't out there, are we ever going to do it right?" But good game-management was never going to be enough. I had to give him end product. Goals. Assists. And I failed to do it.

Even more frustratingly, I had chances in almost every appearance. When you're struggling for a goal, it's easy sometimes to not put yourself forward for the next opportunity. You don't even mean to do it. Often it's sub-conscious. A slight hesitancy arising from a quick 'fight or flight' debate in your mind. At Cambridge, Preecey knew all about this, so would always talk with me about it. "Why weren't you in there?" he'd ask. "Why did you stop? Yeah, you might miss, but you'll never score again if you stop going in there." I learnt to keep going in there. If you miss, you try again.

And that's what I did at Northampton. But unlike at Cambridge, the ball just wouldn't go in. The longer I went without a goal, or even a defining contribution, I felt like I was playing with a knife at my back. The intense desire to do well was offset by anxiety over the possible consequences of doing badly; the feeling of time running out. And in the absence of the proverbial 'one going in off my backside', my nerve clearly failed me.

Around about this time, I remember popping down the shops and seeing a lad in a Northampton shirt with Youngs on the back. It got to me a little bit. I felt really sorry for him, the poor bloke who'd forked out for the name, but it also represented, quite literally, the dreams and ambitions I'd had at the club that would now be left unfulfilled.

Colin pulled me aside after leaving me off the bench one day at Kidderminster. "Clearly you're upset," he said, no doubt reading my oh-so-subtle signals. "Do you want me to circulate your name?" he continued. "We don't want to lose you, you're great to have around the place, with the lads on the bus. But I can see you're not happy." I asked to be put on the list. "I'm here to play football, not cards," is how I remember my response, though that's probably just what I told the lads later. I doubt I said anything quite so sharp in the actual moment.

The first response to my listing came from a familiar source. Chesterfield, up near the play-off zone in Division Two, were managed by Roy McFarland. He invited me up for a few days of training just before Christmas, and said he was happy with what he saw. But as I'd endured such a long period without regular football, he wanted to be sure and would try to arrange a reserve game in the New Year. I returned home to Northampton with renewed enthusiasm.

Four weeks later, I was on my way out of Sixfields. But I wasn't bound for Chesterfield.

League and cup appearances to this point
157 (+56 as sub), 48 goals

14

Free Agent Dowie

In fact, my new destination turned out to be Leyton Orient. Chesterfield was looking less of a sure thing as the days went by, and Rich called to say that Martin Ling, the Orient manager, had come in for me. No sense waiting around for a 'maybe' from Roy when there was a concrete move on the table.

It was effectively a loan initially, to cover a couple of injuries in the Orient squad, but as my contract was running down at Northampton – with no chance of renewal – Orient just took over my existing deal until the end of the season. The O's had impressed me in our 2-2 draw earlier in the season and were still only three points behind the play-off places, despite stuttering form of late. I had next to no idea whether, or indeed how, I would fit in at Brisbane Road. But even if there wasn't a long-term future in the move – and I would be doing my utmost to make sure there was – it had to be better, getting a bit of Football League action again, than sitting on the bench, or even in the stands, at Northampton.

I met up with another Northampton-based player, Lee Steele, for the trip down to the Orient training ground on the Friday. It was a bit of a mud-bath, but from the session it was clear that I would be playing wide right, with the formidable partnership of Steele and Gary Alexander up front. Speaking to Lingy during and after training, I could tell that there was very much an emphasis on the 'wide' part of my job description. He liked an expansive 4-4-2 with genuine width. Real 'chalk on your boots' stuff. I would have to play totally against type. A bit like my first day at Northampton, when the coaches were encouraging the strikers to stay away from me when I really wanted them to come and play, I was left to ponder how much

Lingy or his staff had actually seen me play. But I wasn't about to bring it up in our first meeting. I figured I'd just get on with things and see how they went. Maybe if I played well he might change his grand plan.

My debut the next day was against lowly Notts County. With a big new stand and blocks of flats surrounding the Matchroom Stadium, there was no longer anywhere for players to park their cars. If you were lucky, you could find a spot around the outside of a pretty little park next to the ground. If not, you had to take your chances on one of more foreboding streets nearby. With every chance of a street light being smashed in, leaving your car in complete darkness at night games. Leyton certainly could feel a bit intimidating.

Notts County, though, did not. In even worse form than Orient, it was not a bad game to start with. We were on top almost immediately, and I produced an excellent early cross from which we should have scored. After a bit of a wobble midway through the first half, when County hit our bar, we came out strongly after the break and Andy Scott made up for his earlier miss by chesting down for me to volley into the far corner. After almost two barren years with The Cobblers, I'd almost forgotten what it was like to score. It was such a release, feeling just as good as my first ever goal, for Cambridge at Gillingham, which now seemed an eternity ago.

I came off to warm applause eight minutes from time, and my replacement Donny Barnard sealed a 2-0 victory. Larger-than-life chairman Barry Hearn came into the dressing room in congratulatory mood, saying to me: "I wasn't sure about you in the first half, but what a goal! Changed my mind now." What a goal indeed. It was my first (and would be my last) ever strike from outside the box. Not that it was particularly spectacular. I think it still bounced a couple of times before hitting the net. But hit the net it did. Get in.

That was about as good as it got for me in East London, though. I played another five games from the start and made four appearances from the bench, but, as I suspected from day one, I wasn't what Lingy was looking for in a wide right. He confirmed as much in a good chat we had towards the end of the season. He was full of praise for my attitude and professionalism in training (I was getting a severe sense of déjà vu at this point) but he was after an out-and-out winger. I advised him Shane Tudor would fit the bill, unaware that a deal for Tudes had already been agreed for the summer.

In different circumstances, with different players at his disposal, I think I could have thrived under Lingy. I liked him and was so sad to see his managerial career later cut short by stress-related health issues. I enjoyed training with him, and found him to be very honest, willing to confront anyone – no matter their status in the squad or their relationship with him – that wasn't living up to his expectations. And telling them straight what was lacking.

That can be quite rare in football. Often things get dressed up in vagueness, issues skirted around. Even Colin, who I liked very much, often found it hard to be completely honest in a one-to-one meeting. You could go in after an evaluation of your failings and come out having only seemed to discuss your strengths. However hurt a player may be by a blunt, unflattering assessment of his game, it can only help to crystallise what is required to get in, or stay in, the team. I even got a bit of a volley from Lingy after a quiet first half at Shrewsbury, in only my second game, my debut goal honeymoon period not lasting long at all. But I knew precisely where I stood. Knowing and doing anything about it, though, were miles apart in this instance. I couldn't become a speedy winger overnight. So my time at Orient was up. At least I had a goal to show for it, which is more than could be said for my time at Northampton.

Aside from the goal, and very much enjoying the company of my driving buddy Steeley – despite him nicknaming me 'Dowie' after an unflattering photo of me celebrating my goal on the front of the programme (no offence Iain, but it was meant as an insult! Not that I look like George Clooney, clearly) – there is one thing I remember most from my spell in Leyton: coming on at half-time to replace Andy Scott against Cheltenham. After a poor first period had left us 2-0 down, Lingy was venting his frustrations at the break. Scotty started complaining about having nothing left in the tank and feeling short of breath. Given the situation in the game, the boss was not in the mood to be particularly sympathetic, and, after bringing Scotty off, told him: "Go and get yourself checked out then". If Lingy seemed a touch dismissive of Scotty's claims, he wasn't alone in the dressing room.

The big left-winger had made a few noises about struggling for fitness and feeling lethargic going into games, but there seemed to be a fair bit of scepticism around, the suspicion being that it may be a good smokescreen for ailing form. Far from it. Scotty was quickly diagnosed with hypertrophic cardiomyopathy, the same condition which had caused the death of Marc Vivien-Foe on the pitch two years previously. When a meeting was called, on the Monday morning, for Scotty to break the news of his immediate forced retirement to the lads, there was plenty of guilty feeling palpable in the dressing room. Everyone was just thankful that Scotty was still able to visit us and nothing catastrophic had been allowed to happen.

As the season drew to a close, for the first time, after eight years as a professional, I found myself unattached. A free agent. In the post-Bosman years, thanks to the bountiful moves of Sol Campbell and the like, being a free agent is sometimes seen as a lucrative position. The reality for most, though, is far less glamorous. Those who are free agents not out of choice but because, basically, they are unwanted by their current, soon to be previous, clubs. Every summer, hundreds of these players are tossed into football's swirling summer sink to scrabble around, trying to keep their heads above water and not be dragged down the plug-hole. The majority of them (most having had less than two years as a professional and few, if any, first-team appearances) do not make it out. They are left to, hopefully, earn a few quid in non-League while finding a new way to earn a living.

There should be absolutely no shame in that. If any young players not able to secure a return to the professional ranks have been sensible, taken advantage of the ample education opportunities provided by their scholarship contracts or by the PFA, they can be well-set to find a worthwhile career elsewhere. While also being able to supplement their income, often pretty generously, in the semi-professional game.

But with over 200 Football League appearances to my name and still only 25, I didn't feel quite ready to be cast aside just yet, even though the last two and a bit years had been pretty disastrous. I was confident that there would be a club out there for me. I did have a few worries, though. Would clubs perceive me as an injury risk due to the amount of time I spent on the sidelines at Northampton, not knowing the truth that it was all down to a reasonably minor injury that could and should have been sorted out much faster? While managers might be prepared to accept that I was not Colin Calderwood's cup of tea (though again that assertion would be far from the whole truth), would the subsequent lack of game time at Orient count against me? A second 'failure' in quick succession? Must be something wrong with him, they might think.

This was the first time I'd really needed the help of an agent; to actually keep me in a job rather than just help to negotiate and improve my contract. And Rich was certainly doing his bit. He landed guest slots for me and him (and Wanny, also out of contract after being released by Oxford) on a Radio Five Live chat about the perils of being one of the free agents looking for a new club. Then he arranged an interview with a prominent football website, focusing on possible 'gems' to be found among the victims of the post-season cull. Both gave an opportunity to remind anyone reading or listening of my impressive goal return at Cambridge. Then it was a case of crossing my fingers and waiting for Rich to call. Chelle and I went back home to Mildenhall for a few days to meet up with friends we'd barely seen for a couple of years, and on the way to a restaurant in Cambridge, my phone rang. "Looks like we've got two strong options," said Rich. "Rushden and Bury."

Rushden (& Diamonds, for completists): the upstarts who had roared into the Football League three years earlier on the back of huge benefactor investment. Then went straight up again before the money dried up and they tumbled back down to the lower reaches of the re-branded League Two (still the fourth tier, no matter what number the powers that be ascribed to it).

Bury: a lower mid-table squad full of promise, though much of it had been sold over the previous six months – impressive young strikers David Nugent, Chris Porter and Colin Kazim-Richards all departing. They'd impressed me in all three encounters with Northampton in the previous campaign.

I fancied both sides might be nearer the wrong end of the table than would be ideal (Rushden had finished 22nd and Bury 17th), but I was up for either challenge to retain my place as a Football League professional. On the face of it, Rushden looked the best option. Though Chelle and I had put the house on the market in April in anticipation of having to move, a deal with Diamonds would mean we could stay put, in a house we loved. I'd played against Barry Hunter, the manager (more recently seen as Liverpool's chief scout), in his time as a centre-half at both Rushden and Reading, so I was pretty sure he would know plenty about me as a player. And the facilities at Rushden were second to none in the division. Conversely, Bury was a long way from home (150 miles from Northampton and 205 from Mildenhall, to be exact) and the charms of Gigg Lane were a little more disguised on my visits there; flaky paintwork and grimy dressing rooms were my abiding memories. But no sooner had I stated my preference than Rushden started to go cold on the idea. So I looked to be heading oop North. Surely it couldn't be that grim up there.

While Chelle kept the house looking spick and span for another spate of viewings from prospective buyers, Rich and I journeyed up the M6, around the M60 and then up the M66 to meet up with Bury manager Graham Barrow and chairman Ian Harrop. After 20 minutes or so of general small-talk, we split into pairs so Graham and I could discuss football while the others thrashed out some figures. Graham did his best to convince me that, though I'd seen in the press that a deal for

Macclesfield forward Matt Tipton had been hijacked at the last minute by Carlton Palmer's Mansfield, I was by no means a fall-back option. My versatility made me more desirable, apparently. I liked Graham (and not just because of that complimentary white lie). He spoke in quite a soft and welcoming manner, and made a lot of sense as he broached the pros and cons of the various systems he had used at times during the previous campaign. And why he thought, with the additions he was making to the squad – including Allan Smart and Stuart Barlow, the experienced front men – the top half was a possibility for a club still at a distinct disadvantage financially, having been only rescued by bucket collections and a drive for donations a few years before. I certainly got the impression of a man I'd be happy to work with.

As Ian and Rich concluded their discussions, Ian and Graham made their exit and left me and Rich to chew things over. I was pressing for a two-year deal – which would give me and Chelle the security to invest in a house – and while I knew that the money would be a drop from The Cobblers, I was hoping to avoid a calamitous one. Bury, spooked by my long injury lay-off and a lack of game-time in the previous two years, were much too cautious for that. They could offer me an acceptable financial package of £800 per week, but only if their initial commitment was limited to six months, so I could prove my fitness. Otherwise they could stretch to a full year on reduced terms of around £650 to £700 per week. There was a broad gentleman's agreement that if I did prove my fitness, the six-month deal would be extended to the end of the season on the same higher-rate terms, or even extended at the same level by a further year if things had gone particularly well. Always keen to back myself, I agreed to go for the option with shorter-term guarantees but what I saw as better long-term prospects.

I went back home to tell Chelle, who informed me that the couple who'd come round for a second viewing on the house had opted not to make an offer. They were the second couple to tease us by coming back for a second time before withdrawing their interest. While our estate agent prepared to tell us we needed to drop the price after 10 unsuccessful viewings, we started to look at rental prices in the Bury area. With only six months guaranteed, buying a house would not be an option.

League and cup appearances to this point
163 (+60 as sub), 49 goals

15

Fifteen Weeks to Save a Football Career

A week after Rich and I had met Graham and Ian, Chelle and I stayed the night at the same Village hotel, ahead of the start of pre-season training the following day. What I didn't know at that point was that the club had only booked us in for one night, and with a Coldplay gig at the nearby Reebok stadium the next night, every hotel around was booked solid.

The closest we could find with a room available was a run-down relic called Scaitcliffe Hall, 18 miles away in Todmorden over the Yorkshire border. Having just about managed to haul my little Peugeot 206 up and down the steepest hill I'd ever seen (we don't really do hills in Suffolk, you see) to get to and from the hotel, fortunately I was able to block-book the Village on club discount rates for the next couple of weeks. Which provided a base for me to get to training easily and for us to start checking out rentals in the surrounding area. We ended up 'living' in the Village for almost four weeks in total before finding somewhere suitable.

Meanwhile, I was trying to impress as pre-season started in earnest. The schedule was a kind of halfway house between the new world, scientific approach I'd enjoyed at Cambridge, and the old-school, distance running-based method I'd hated – despite my proficiency allowing me to show up well – in my first year at Northampton. There was plenty of ball-work involved, during which Graham appeared to be settling on a 3-man backline with the experienced captain Dave Challinor (he of the famous long throw) as the organiser-in-chief.

I looked to be competing with Stuey Barlow for a spot

alongside Smarty, our target man, up front. But any competition was seriously short-lived. In our second friendly against Bradford, my right ankle was crunched in a tackle in the second half and I had to limp off. It wasn't quite on the scale of my ankle sprain at Tranmere for The Cobblers, but it was certainly bad enough to write off the next four warm-up games.

Impact injuries are one of football's lotteries, largely unpreventable save for jumping out of tackles, and this was just plain bad luck. Following on from Northampton, where I felt injuries had derailed me before I could even come close to establishing myself, it was extremely frustrating watching all the lads forward their claims to a place in the starting line-up while I was stuck up in the stands. As a consequence, I declared myself fit for our final friendly at home to Bolton when I was far from it.

I got Joe Hinnigan, our physio, to strap the ankle as strongly as possible, but I was still in a lot of pain as I warmed up at half-time. I had to grit my teeth. I just couldn't let the season get underway without having had at least a few minutes to show what I could bring to the table. I enjoyed a lively cameo in the second half, skipping past Nicky Hunt with a nifty bit of footwork at one point, then playing a part in our winning goal. I was playing with a constant grimace, but I'd always been happy to play through pain if that's all it was. Here, it was a bit more than that. The ankle was still pretty flimsy, so there was certainly an increased chance of going over on it and causing a more severe injury. But with only six months to prove my fitness, I didn't want to waste any more time. And I came through it unscathed, just about.

As I'd already missed a large part of pre-season, though, Graham was not convinced of my readiness for action. Due to lack of numbers, I did make the bench for the first two games of the season, getting a short time on the pitch in both. But with a fuller squad thereafter, I was back in the stands for a few games.

I was still working on re-strengthening the ankle every morning and it was while hopping on a trampette that I caught a sight which made my heart sink. Breezing past with Graham was Matt Tipton, the striker who'd chosen Mansfield over Bury to open the door for me only a couple of months earlier. But after enduring a torrid eight weeks with Carlton Palmer, Tippy had begged Graham to rescue him, and the manager was only too keen to snap up a player whose 33 goals in the previous two seasons had helped transform Macclesfield briefly from strugglers into play-off contenders.

So now I was fifth in line for a first-team spot up front. I'd barely had 20 minutes on the pitch yet and here was another striker to immediately usurp me in the pecking order. Tippy scored a great goal on his debut as well. I could only try to show my best in training and hope someone would notice. I'd always been someone who took training seriously and worked hard, whatever we were being asked to do; it was the best way to regain fitness and confidence. Graham had drafted in former Wigan and Tranmere boss Ray Mathias as an extra coach, so there was fresh pair of eyes to try to impress. And it seemed to be starting to work.

After two narrow defeats left us dangerously close to the bottom of the league, Graham called everyone together for a bit of a call to arms before training. He started to point a few fingers, mainly at the new signings he felt were not pulling their weight, in training or in games. I was only mentioned in dispatches, as others such as Smarty (who'd got himself sent off for elbowing against Leicester in the League Cup) bore the brunt, but still I went to knock on Graham's door after the session.

"I hold my hands up to a poor game at Carlisle in the ressies a couple of weeks ago," I said. "But I've been training well. Scoring goals and making goals. I want a chance to show you out on the pitch." Graham replied that he wasn't really aiming any of his barbs at me. "You *have* been showing up well in training, me and Ray were just saying that," he said. "I just think you've been short of football in the last couple of years, and you missed a lot of pre-season, so you need to get more training and more games under your belt before you're ready." At least he'd seen enough to get me back on the bench for the next game, which avoided the embarrassment of returning to Northampton to sit in the stands.

We managed a creditable 1-1 draw with the promotion favourites, despite having ten men for the last 25 minutes. But decent result or not, it still meant one win in eight League games. And with a basement battle at home to Boston to follow, there was a sense around the dressing room and the local press that the knives were out for Graham if we didn't come out on top. When we conceded another late equaliser, there were plenty of murmurings of discontent from the stands. And on the Monday, Graham's departure was confirmed.

A bit like towards the end of Roy's reign at Cambridge, I could feel that some of the lads – ones who the boss had backed and kept faith with – so desperately wanted him to keep his job that they became anxious and risk-averse in their play. Never more was it true than in those last two games: grimly trying to hold on to 1-0 leads, forgetting to keep constructing attacks, dropping ever deeper, eventually succumbing. As sorry as I felt for Graham, though – he was certainly one of football's good guys, and I was so pleased to see him become an integral part of Wigan's success under Roberto Martinez – I was far more concerned with my own situation.

It felt like my world was falling apart. Graham was the man who'd persuaded me to uproot myself and Chelle and move so far from home, family and friends. He was the one who'd stressed that the six-month contract was just to protect the club against my injury history, and that if I stayed fit it would be extended. And after a difficult start, our recent chat made me feel like I was finally starting to make a better impression. But with Graham gone, and having struggled thus far to make any real impact at all, I was just a nobody with only 15 weeks left on my deal. Easy to jettison for any new manager intent on re-building the squad in his image.

We weren't actually in at the ground for training on the day the decision was made public. Well, not those of us in the reserves, anyway. We had a Monday night fixture at local rivals Rochdale. Youth team manager Chris Casper was in charge. He was also, for at least the immediate future, in caretaker charge of the first team.

Neither of those facts filled me with confidence. My only dealing with Chris had been when he took charge of that awful reserve game at Carlisle, the one I'd felt the need to apologise for to Graham. Nothing had gone right for me that night as a Glenn Murray-inspired home side dominated us completely. So I didn't think my stock with Chris was particularly high at this point. And feeling an intense need to impress didn't do much for my game in the first half at Spotland. I was mired in double-think, my natural instincts overpowered by thoughts of how best to do something noteworthy, memorable, something to get me a first-team shot. 'Trying too hard' is how it's often described in football.

Chris gave me and Stuart Barlow – the only experienced members of the team – a bit of a dressing-down at the interval. Mercifully, things did improve in the second period, and I ended up scoring the winner (though I nearly managed to bounce that chance over an open goal from about three yards). But I didn't think I'd played myself any closer to the first team.

I was on the bench for Chris's first game at Oxford, coming on late to provide an assist for our goal in a 2-1 defeat, but the next two weeks were the lowest in my entire footballing life. I was left out of the squad for the games against Bristol Rovers (a win!) and Lincoln, before travelling to Hyde to take on Manchester United reserves in some local cup competition. It was a chastening experience. With Guiseppe Rossi practically untouchable for our youthful side, and Danny Simpson so strong and quick at right-back against me when we occasionally got the ball out of our half, I've never felt so down after a game. It felt like men against boys, but at 26 I was supposed to be one of the men, not the boys.

The post-match debrief inevitably focused on the failure of our three front men – me, Tippy and Stuey – to help out the bunch of kids behind them getting the run-around. "What is there, six or seven hundred League games between you? And you gave us, and these boys, nothing," was the withering assessment from physio Joe, quickly backed up by Chris. Tippy and Stuey both piped up defensively, playing the 'we're up against Man United' card. "This isn't Man United," Joe came back. "Half of these boys will end up in the lower leagues, Championship at best. And they're still only learning at the moment. Don't kid yourself." The fact that his argument would, in the future, be slightly undermined by Gerard Pique's collection of La Liga, Champions League, European Championship and World Cup winner's medals didn't really matter. I certainly wasn't going to argue because he had a point.

On the minibus back I was in a seriously philosophical, contemplative mood. Did I still have what it took? I'd always backed my ability to show any manager I was a good footballer, even if, for whatever reason, they couldn't fit me into their team. But after that night, I really wasn't sure I could with Chris. Which was a problem as his good start was about to see him given the job permanently.

I actually had a lot of time for him. I thought he was a good coach. I agreed with a lot of what he said, in training and during games. I thought his early emphasis on fitness was welcome and effective. But he could also come across as officious and dour. A bit mirthless.

On Fridays, the Bury version of the yellow jersey was that the worst trainer had to pop to the shop over the road and buy biscuits for the boys to share with their post-session cuppa. Pretty harmless, but Chris signalled his dislike for it. "Could we not buy fruit instead?" he asked, provoking a few smirks and rolled eyes. So the lads used to hide the biscuits. Then one day, he accidentally stumbled upon a pack of shortbread when he knocked over the tactics board. "What's this?" he fumed. "All f***** butter?!" And threw the pack down on the floor, shattering the biscuits. Already younger than half the team, such outbursts over trivial matters could only make him look like a stroppy teenager. Or someone used to dealing with kids in the youth team.

The art of football management can be complex. Football knowledge is a given, but you need a strange alchemy of gravitas and charisma to get your ideas – however valid they may be – across to the players. These qualities can take time to develop, and even then they are not always transferable – often a manager can be highly successful at one club but struggle at another. It can depend on the personalities in each dressing room and how receptive they are to a certain style. Chris didn't yet command the requisite amount of respect to throw a wobbly about biscuits, as no doubt his mentor Sir Alex Ferguson could have pulled off on many occasions.

But Chris was still managing to get ideas across well enough. The fabled new manager effect was certainly in evidence. It's easy to put that down to players upping their effort levels to impress the new man, and there may be something in that theory. Well-established players want to make sure they retain their places. Players previously out of the picture eye an opportunity for a fresh start. But it's not quite that straightforward – more important than any perceived increase in work ethic are the new ideas, the focus on different things in training. In this instance, Chris restored a back four pretty quickly and then drilled the 'two banks of four' set-up in training. It definitely made us more solid.

The next game was at Rushden away on a Friday night. I spied a rare opportunity to get back home for the weekend, which I felt would provide a much-needed pick-me-up. So I knocked on Chris's door to ask to be excused from Saturday's training session (a warm-down for those who'd played, a bit more for those who hadn't). As I'd got his attention for a few minutes, I thought I'd go a bit further and ask him why he'd given others a chance so far and not me.

"I don't think any of the strikers have been great so far and I think I deserve a shot just as much as any of them," I said, trying to sound as assertive as possible. I knew I didn't really have a leg to stand on. He'd seen me play three times and, but for 20 minutes or so at Rochdale, I'd been distinctly average. Well, not even average, actually. But I just felt I needed to speak to him to show him that I still really wanted it. I still cared. I wasn't resigned to being released (not quite yet).

I sat in the stands with Chelle at Rushden and watched us win convincingly. We were starting to look like a team. A pretty decent team. But a team with no place for me. Then, near the end, both our strikers, Smarty and Jon Newby, went down with serious-looking injuries. Awful for the boys, but a crumb of hope for me.

The next week, I did return to the bench, but Nicky Adams, not quite 19 and a winger in the youth team under Chris, was given a start in a slightly unfamiliar role up front with Tippy. He scored a very well-taken goal, which proved to be the winner. The Tuesday after provided what I saw as my last-chance saloon. Conference side Halifax away in the LDV Trophy. If I couldn't show Chris what I was made of in this game, I didn't think I'd get another chance. My contract was up in ten weeks' time.

Ten minutes in, Halifax – a good footballing side – passed their way through us and Craig Dootson – our number two goalkeeper making his first competitive appearance for the club – upended the on-rushing striker to bring a penalty and a red card. Sensing that I was in danger of being substituted for the replacement keeper, I sprinted over to the bench to talk over the plan with the gaffer. I thought my desire to be part of the discussion might keep me on the pitch. Wrong. Chris just apologised and asked me to sit down in the dugout, leaving Stuey alone up front. And that was where I thought my Bury career would effectively end. Stewing on the bench for 75 minutes or so at the Shay. What a way to go.

As Halifax banged in goal after goal (it ended 6-1), however, I started to get the feeling of a lucky escape. And as Chris charged around the dressing room afterwards, venting his spleen (and smashing a mirror into the bargain), my disappointment at seeing possibly my last chance slipping away turned to relief. At least I wasn't tainted by having been part of such a wretched display.

I was still not at the front of the queue, though. When Tippy's hernia problem ruled him out, only Stuey and I were left as strikers within the squad. But in Thursday's training session,

Brian Barry-Murphy, normally a deep-lying midfield playmaker or occasional left-back, was selected to partner Nicky up top. Then, on our superb training facility at Goshen public playing fields – we used to dub it 'The Swamp' – Murphs went over badly on his ankle. So Chris was out of options. On the Friday, pretty much by default, I was in the team.

As we entered Chester's Deva Stadium – where I'd played my first full 90 minutes for Cambridge seven years previously – it felt as if I'd been awarded a free hit, like in cricket after a no-ball. I couldn't see how I could get any lower in Chris's estimations if he was prepared to play two people out of position instead of give me a game. And I felt pretty confident walking out to play. While I might have been put through the mill recently, the team were playing well; unbeaten in four, three of them wins. We had good full-backs, in Tom Kennedy and Paul Scott, who I thought would spot my runs and deliver accordingly. My optimism was well-founded. We started the game well and took the lead early. I nearly got on the end of David Buchanan's whipped cross, but behind me Dwayne Mattis arrived to head home.

I had a decent game. Not amazing. Not earth-shatteringly good. But decent. Held the ball up well, brought our midfield into play well. We looked to be quite comfortable heading into the final stages before our goalkeeper Neil Edwards misjudged a long ball and ended up bringing down Michael Branch for a penalty. But despite the dropped two points, I was pleased with my day's work.

With Tippy back for the following week, I returned to the bench. But just before the hour mark, shortly after we'd gone 3-0 down, the gaffer asked me to get ready. In a rather bizarre exchange on the touchline while we waited for a break in play, Chris apologised for not starting me. "You did well for me last week and I should have stayed with it," he said. "And I know your contract's up soon. Don't worry about that, I'm sorting it." Buoyed by the unexpected news, I helped us recover to 3-2, though we were still beaten eventually. For the first time since arriving at Bury, I felt a genuine, useful member of the squad.

I came on wide left at Mansfield next time out and cleared

one off the line (there's a first time for everything!), before stealing possession and teeing up new loan signing Danny Reet for our third in a comprehensive 3-0 win. I started the next two in wide positions, earning a painful bloody nose/double-black eye combo in a hard-fought draw at Barnet. Though the return of David Flitcroft ('Flicker') from suspension meant I was soon sub again, I made a real contribution as we produced a coupon-busting double, beating second-placed Orient away and unbeaten leaders Wycombe at home.

On the bus back from the former, Scotty paid me the ultimate compliment for a player of my type. "It's so easy playing with Youngsie," he said to a couple of the lads. "You look up and he's just always there, available." I'd always seen that as the foundation of my game when playing as a striker, and if that was going well, the goals would normally follow. The Wycombe win (in which I'd come on after only 15 minutes) brought up 21 points from Chris's 11 games in charge. We were now seven points away from the drop-zone and looked upwardly mobile.

As we trained on Christmas morning, I'd just signed my contract extension until the end of the season, I was in the team, and everything was rosy. After the Orient game, Steeley had said he was pleased to see me looking so relaxed and happy. But no sooner had I started to feel at home than things started to go wrong for us.

Simon Whaley was sold to Preston for £250,000, thus stripping us of our top scorer and his ability to carry the ball many yards at pace, helping us turn defence into attack with ease. A major outlet no longer available.

Reety's loan ended. He wasn't a world-beater and had the worst body shape of just about any footballer the lads had ever seen. But he was a passable target man, complemented me quite well when we played together and could certainly sniff out a goal – scoring four in six League games.

Our back four, marshalled by veterans Challi and Colin Woodthorpe ('Woodie'), suddenly looked vulnerable. We had looked imperious, conceding only eight times in 11 games. Maybe it was the loss of players at the top end making it harder to get out which caused the problem, but we conceded 17 in the next seven.

We kicked off the New Year with two pastings, 4-1 at Peterborough and 4-0 at title-chasing Carlisle. In the latter, out of sheer frustration and for the first time ever, I deliberately launched into a tackle from behind when I knew I had no chance of winning the ball. I took the man and received a deserved yellow card. I think I wanted to at least look like I was trying to do something. After working so hard, since that ghastly night against Manchester United, to get back into the picture and earn my continued employment, I didn't want to return to those feelings of hopelessness.

But, when the next game rolled around, I was left out. Not just of the starting 11 but of the entire 16. I was gutted and angry. I certainly hadn't been worse than anyone else in the two games; I was actually quite lively in the first half at Peterborough. But I had to start to accept that I had less margin for error than the other forwards.

If that sounds unfair, it wasn't. It was common sense. The management staff may have loved it when I was dropping cleverly into holes, bringing others into play, helping us to break teams down. But if I was slightly off my game, I offered no plan B. If you're a big man and your touch is letting you down, you can still provide an aerial target, both for clearances and for crosses. Even while having a torrid time you can still influence the game easily enough. If you've got pace and things aren't working into feet, you can still provide an outlet to help a wayward clearance become a penetrative through-ball. You can still turn a game, even when not at your best. So when things aren't going well, managers are understandably more likely to play the percentages and select the obvious game-changers. So I found myself edged out by Jake Speight (quick), the returning Jon Newby (quick) and the new loanee from Sheffield United, Colin Marrison (quick and tall). I had to do better.

Of course, if I'd scored goals (or even one) I could have forced his hand. But they hadn't come. At Peterborough, having been denied by a good save and goal-line clearance early on, I even missed a late freebie as Challi scuffed one towards goal following a corner. All I had to do was tap it in, but I kicked thin air. Granted, I distracted the man on the line so the ball rolled in anyway, but I could have really done with the goal myself.

When Newbs succumbed to injury again I got back on the bench, but it took an impressive outing in the ressies against Burnley – played at Accrington, where the changing rooms looked like a death trap, with water leaking through the ceiling into the electrics! – to get me another chance from the start. We'd dropped to within a couple of points of the bottom two.

We travelled to Rochdale for a local derby, almost certain that the game would be called off. The pitch was frozen. But somehow the ref deemed it playable, and I was glad he did, as I opened my account for the Shakers in the second half, getting across a defender to tuck in a flicked-on long throw. A contentious penalty decision against our new loan signing, Kasper Schmeichel, enabled Rickie Lambert to equalise. That dampened my celebrations a bit, but the goal was still a real boon for my confidence.

I was a fixture in the side for the next two months, combining well with another loan frontman, Jon Daly ('Dints'). I only managed one further goal, a sweet left foot strike after charging down a clearance from the Rochdale goalkeeper, Matty Gilks, in the return local derby at Gigg Lane. But on top of the qualities I knew Chris now appreciated in me, I consistently displayed a goal threat, hitting the post three times aside from the two goals. That was enough to keep me in the team. On merit, not by default. Until Big Ron Manager came to town.

The perma-tanned one arrived at Gigg Lane with the Sky cameras in tow for his management troubleshooter documentary. The full extent of his orange-ness was only clear when a fire alarm forced us to evacuate the ground. Soon I would wish we'd not been allowed back in. I just had a complete nightmare. Everything that had gone right in recent weeks went wrong. The ball was going under my foot. My touch was heavy. My lay-offs were going behind people. Dints alongside me had a beast as well.

The gaffer put it down to a bad day at the office and picked us both again the next week at Lincoln. But though I couldn't get any worse, I wasn't much better. I deservedly lost my place in the side. Assistant manager Ian Miller ('Dusty') noted my disappointment when the team was set up in training. "You've been important for us for the last ten games, but it just hasn't been there in the last two," he offered in his Scottish burr by way of explanation. But I already knew that. Any annoyance was at myself, not anyone else. To make matters worse, where we had pulled five points away from the relegation zone and looked poised to stretch that gap, we were now back within three points. We headed up to Darlington's white elephant of a stadium knowing that defeat would leave us in grave danger of dropping out of the Football League.

In such a serious situation, the most uncomfortably hilarious thing happened after eight minutes. You've probably seen it on *A Question of Sport's* 'What Happened Next?' Chris Brass, the experienced right-back brought in from York in January, positioned himself under a high ball dropping about eight yards from our goal. Attempting to clear the ball over his shoulder, he succeeded only in belting it into his own face – breaking his nose in the process – and it flashed past a disbelieving Kasper in goal.

Tippy and I sprinted from the bench to 'warm up' as quickly as possible so we could burst out laughing without offending the gaffer, sat in the stand behind. We could hardly be seen to be cracking up at a goal that could end up relegating us. It was just so funny, though. And it didn't help that Darlo mercilessly repeated the incident at breaks in play on their jumbo screens in the corners. Cue outbursts of laughter every time from the sparsely-populated stands. Thankfully, Flicker blasted in an equaliser from 25 yards midway through the half. At which point, Dusty could afford a chuckle with the lads about Brassy's blunder.

With ten minutes left, though, the laughter ran out as we went 2-1 down. If the score had stayed that way, we would have been joint third-bottom, hovering over the precipice, with two games to play. But Murphs curled in a free-kick before Tippy tapped home from a corner (thanks to some terrible goalkeeping from Sam Russell – why couldn't he have done that when I was trying to get my first goal for Northampton?!).

We were now one win from safety, and I almost scored the goal to seal the deal against Mansfield. The ball broke for me six yards out on the angle, but Alex John-Baptiste made a superb sliding block. It left us needing one point from our last game at Notts County, where, quite amazingly, we were one of seven sides – including our opponents – that could possibly fill the second relegation slot, alongside Rushden.

With almost 10,000 fans present, it was a high-pressure, nerve-shredding atmosphere. I entered the fray on the hour, with us leading by a Dwayne Mattis header. Ten minutes from time, I read the trajectory of Challi's clearance while the defence were distracted by Tippy retreating from offside, finding myself clean through. As Kevin Pilkington came out, I found a moment of calm to slip the ball between his legs and send our fans behind the goal into raptures. We were safe.

Suddenly games of Chinese whispers were breaking out all over the stands and the pitch. Oxford, the team starting the day in pole position for the drop, were apparently in front. 1-0. 2-0. If true, defeat could relegate County, so they piled forward. (In actual fact, Oxford were never in front on their way to the 3-2 defeat to Orient that sealed their fate.) Having grabbed one back, they equalised in the last minute when Kasper made a rare slip, conceding a penalty trying to recover his initial fumble. Both teams could breathe a huge sigh of relief at the final whistle. The superb travelling fans behaved like we'd just won the league, invading the pitch and waiting (loudly) for the squad to re-appear in the directors' box, cheering us one last time before making their way home.

I felt great that night, but I still wasn't sure if my coolly-taken goal – which was ultimately meaningless in the relegation battle, but seemed crucial at the time – would help to land me a new contract or merely end up a fond farewell. The lads met up for a few beers the next day, watching the final day of the Premier League in the pub, with over half of us not to find out our future until meetings organised for the Monday morning.

League and cup appearances to this point
179 (+74 as sub), 52 goals

16

The Defensive Forward

After a celebratory night – where centre-half John Fitzgerald earned the nickname 'Beermats' after a Guinness-fuelled vomiting attack left him looking like he'd been chowing down on them – it was judgment day. I honestly expected to be thanked for my efforts and sent on my way, to find pastures new. I'd had plenty of good moments in those last three months of the season, but I wasn't too confident my overall contribution would be reckoned worthy of another contract.

We already knew, via Brassy, that the York striker, Andy Bishop – one of the Conference's hottest properties – had agreed to sign. Therefore I was surprised, but nonetheless delighted, when Chris, sat alongside Ian Harrop, said he wanted to offer me a new deal. He'd been impressed with me over the last few months, he went on, and he thought I could score goals on a more regular basis if we got the attacking function of the team sorted out. Ian then moved on to the finer details, saying I'd have to take a cut from £40,000 a year to around £34,000. But I wasn't bothered about that. It was still a decent salary. I just wanted the chance to establish myself at a club again, as I had at Cambridge.

All players are different, just as all human beings are, but I always felt that you can only produce your absolute best when you feel comfortable and respected at a club, by your team-mates and the management staff. When you don't need to worry that every mistake or every bad game will see them try to replace you. That gives you the freedom to try things, to avoid playing it safe, without fear. I'm not trying to pooh-pooh competition for places. The pressure to be better than your peers is what has driven everyone who makes the grade as a professional from a very young age. They're used to it, and it's the natural order of things. If someone is doing your job better than you, you expect they will take your place. But being able to prove your worth and subsequently earn a little bit of respite when you – inevitably – have small dips in form, is also key.

Some will see it differently. They want players constantly on the edge. How many times have you heard fans complain that a player has started to perform out of his skin only when his contract is coming to an end and he needs to earn another one? That heightened sense of urgency might bring an increased desire that transforms a player's form. But I don't think those heightened states are sustainable for long.

On the flip-side, the complaint is sometimes that a player has gone off the boil the minute he's signed a substantial new deal. Some players do appear to get lazy when comfortable. You'll hear plenty of grumbling around dressing rooms that 'so-and-so will always stay in the side, no matter how bad he is'. Often that's more reflective of denial on the part of the accusers, refusing to acknowledge that their own form has been underwhelming or that the player they're lambasting offers something valued by the management. But sometimes it's valid. If a player seems to have lost his edge, it's up to good man-management to recognise and combat that.

Like I said, everyone's different and requires motivating differently. But I know my professional pride and self-esteem wouldn't allow me to drop my standards or work-rate regardless of whether I was signed up for one year on peanuts or ten years on a fat salary. They drove me more than any other factor. Which is why I despair somewhat when I hear a lot of armchair punditry bemoaning young lads being given too much too soon, in reference to the astronomical sums being offered to teenagers by the big clubs.

Of course it's easy to surmise, if those players don't make as much of themselves as expected, that it was the huge early rewards that derailed them. Depending on their personality and upbringing, both in a private and footballing sense, it may have a negative effect on some. But if, as I believe, the true drivers of success come from within, then those rewards won't make a jot of difference. Whether young players are given enough opportunities to break through at the top level these days is a separate and compelling argument, and I'd be more worried about that than the financial side. For the ones who really have the potential to go far, no matter how much money they earn, they'll continue to strive for improvement and perfection. Neither Steven Gerrard nor Frank Lampard seemed to struggle for motivation to keep progressing, even when earning in one month what many won't earn in a lifetime.

With my new contract signed and sealed, Chelle and I started house-hunting. I didn't see the value of wasting £600 a month on rent when I could be investing it in property and paying off a mortgage. I was not blasé, thinking it was guaranteed that I would now become part of the furniture at Bury and play at Gigg Lane for years. But I reasoned that in the football hot-bed of the North West, there were so many clubs within a stone's throw that, even if Bury released me, I could find somewhere else close enough.

We loved living in Tottington village (a fact that always raised a jokey 'oooooh!' from Bury's very likeable groundsman, Mike Curtis, who'd grown up near the ground – it was nice but not a gated community or anything too posh). And we loved being so close to Manchester, a vibrant city full of culture and still developing. In hindsight, it was a mistake to buy a house, given the events I will go on to describe, but we were very happy to find a lovely three-bed semi in (ironically enough) Calderwood Close, which we of course referred to as Colin.

Infuriatingly, I picked up another minor injury – a groin pull – in pre-season, which meant I missed the first two games of the new season. I was decorating the front room of our new house, listening to our opening match at Milton Keynes on the radio. It sounded like we put up a decent show before losing to a late goal. But pretty crushing defeats against Chester, Shrewsbury and Wycombe (in which Sky Sports News, again, reported me – a late substitute on my return from injury – as being sent off, leading to another flurry of curious texts) left the gaffer searching for solutions.

I tried to offer one in our reserve game at Preston. Our new assistant manager, replacing Dusty, was former Sunderland left-back Martin Scott. So far, due to the injury, the only contact I'd had with him were his jokes about my pale bare chest reminding him he needed to buy milk. This was my first chance to impress him on the pitch. Not that I got off to the greatest start.

The team minibus, obviously realising that the departure time specified by goalkeeping coach Ian Willcock would be cutting it fine, left Gigg Lane early. I (along with the young right-back Damien Quigley, as it transpired) was left to make my own way to Deepdale as soon as possible. I got there with, I hoped, about 30 seconds to spare, but Scotty was none too pleased. Realising it was not the time or place to relate what had happened, I just got ready for the match.

Once we were out on the pitch, things got a bit better. I played well and scored in a 3-1 victory. After coming on to good effect in our surprise Carling Cup win over Championship Sunderland, I was in the side for the visit of Grimsby. So was Kasper, returning on loan to replace the experienced Alan Fettis ('Fetts') in goal. Unusually, it was with two headers from corners that I set us on our way to a 3-0 win. A week later we went to a well-fancied Peterborough side and, after a solid all-round display, nicked the points with a late penalty.

The promise of those wins faded as Bish, who was still finding his feet at the club and with whom I was just starting to build a rapport, injured his knee in our next game. When he returned, two games later, I was forced off early at Hereford after my wrist was crushed, sandwiched between two challenging opponents. Luckily it wasn't broken, but I'd never before realised how important a wrist is for an outfield player – for balance and holding off opponents. As I tried to soldier on through the pain for half an hour that day, it was agony every time an opponent came near. I think an ankle sprain would have been easier to play through. Three 1-0 defeats, all where we had chances to merit at least a draw, saw us drop back into the bottom two.

I missed the next game and by the time I returned, with a

ridiculous-looking soft cast to protect other players from the support required on my wrist, Chris had brought in a new striker, Glynn Hurst, on loan from Notts County. Hursty had scored a hat-trick past us for Notts the season before. He was a seasoned goal-getter with good pace and a superb leap. He scored five in his first five, and after a couple of draws we won six on the bounce to climb the table. Then Hursty's initial loan was up and, in order for him to miss the fewest number of games before we could make his move permanent in January, he was unavailable for our home game with Bristol Rovers. A chance for me.

I, and we – befitting a team in such good form – started on the front foot and I was playing a full part in our domination when, just 18 minutes in, I latched onto a loose ball on the edge of the box and tried to shoot. A defender got a foot in front of the ball to block and my knee jarred completely, damaging my patella tendon. As desperately as I tried to run off the problem, Nicky Reid the physio rightly called time on my involvement after a few quick tests. I was helped off, so disappointed to have lost my chance to take advantage of Hursty's absence, and watched as we continued to boss the game only to be hit with two late sucker-punches to lose 2-0.

The gaffer tried to keep my chin up, saying that I'd looked sharp and that if I'd stayed on at the same level, he would have probably kept me in the side even when Hursty was back. But even if that was true, rather than him just trying to be supportive, it was irrelevant now. I hadn't stayed on. I hadn't been able to supplant Hursty. It was the first time in my career I felt truly hard-done by. Completely beholden to luck. Or fate, if you're more spiritually-inclined. Call it what you want.

Anyone who has read the insightful writing of Matthew Syed in *The Times,* or the excellent work of the American academic Malcolm Gladwell on the nature of success, will know just how much of our lives are dictated by luck, or randomness. In football, for individuals, that can mean injuries. For teams, it can mean the goalkeeper of another team having his best game of the season against you, and then chucking in two when he faces one of your rivals. The randomness is not under your control. All you can do is take advantage of the opportunities that do come your way, the things that are under your control. This is what the best do. Time after time. Obviously I couldn't always manage it.

But acknowledging that some things are beyond your control doesn't make those uncontrollables any less exasperating. I'd not done anything wrong here. In the four-and-a-half games I'd played, I'd played well. I'd scored a couple of goals. I was developing a partnership with Bish, who was ready to catch fire. The team was getting better. But then two freak impact injuries (not soft tissue, not indicative of being at all unfit) left me a spectator while Hursty came in and made hay, scoring eight in 15 games before Christmas. I can't guarantee that I would have scored the same amount of goals. But the frustration is in the opportunity being taken from you purely by a couple of chance collisions.

While I was laid off, Chris understandably moved to bring in another forward option for the bench. Matty Blinkhorn, 21, from Blackpool had plenty of talent and presence. There was a short piece in the *Bury Times* to herald his arrival. The gaffer came in reading it the next day, intrigued by the byline. It read: 'by Tom Youngs'. Having started a Sports Journalism degree, promoted and part-funded by the PFA under the guidance of former Sheffield Wednesday defender Lawrie Madden at Staffordshire University, I'd arranged a work placement at the local paper. I hadn't expected to be credited with a story on my first night there (I didn't actually interview Blinks, I just wrote a piece based on the quotes the main reporter had recorded), so hadn't yet mentioned it to Chris. Luckily for me, he was smiling as he read it out. He knew me well enough to know I'd cause him no problems. Woodie was particularly amused by my description of Blinks as 'rangy'.

I was able to land the work placement because I had a good relationship with Marc Iles, who reported on Bury for the paper. But then I had a good relationship with the local reporters at all my clubs. I could never understand why some players were so unforthcoming in dealing with the press. In the Premier League, fair enough, you might fear saying the wrong thing or being misquoted and causing a big news story. And maybe coverage of that has made all footballers completely distrustful of journalists. The hatchet men. But in the lower leagues, I could see only benefits.

If you're trying to advance your career by moving up the League ladder, keeping the local press onside can only help in ensuring lots of positive reviews being published and attracting wider attention. And closer to home, local reporters wield a lot of influence on the supporters of smaller clubs.

All Premier League games will either be shown live on TV or have extensive highlights broadcast, and be covered in detail by a vast array of papers and online media. Every tiny action from the game is known to the world. But at Bury, for example, the only in-depth reporting on a game (aside from a live radio broadcast) was from the *Bury Times*. If, say, about 500 fans made the long trip to Torquay, out of a fan-base totalling around 5,000 who came on at least a semi-regular basis, the *Bury Times* report is the main source of information on the game, and how the players performed, for around 90% of supporters. It can be an important factor in public opinion. So I always thought it best to be a friend, not an enemy, of the writer of those reports. When you're the star of the show, he'll write about it no matter what he thinks of you, but when things aren't going so well, maybe he'll be less inclined to really put the boot in if you've always been amiable and available.

Marc couldn't write me back into the squad, though. I recovered from the knee injury pretty quickly, but Blinks had already become Chris's bench-warmer of choice, alongside Speighty. After a couple of weeks in the stands, despite showing up well and scoring in the reserves, I went to see the gaffer in his office to plead my case. "I'm happy with what you're doing," he assured me. "But Bish and Hursty are on fire and I like to keep Speighty on the bench for his pace and Blinks for his size. Your chance will come again, I'm sure," he added, before informing me that his dad, former Burnley manager Frank, was a fan of mine and had also been asking why I wasn't involved. I'm sure he was just making conversation, but it didn't make me feel any better about being out of the squad.

On Boxing Day, after a draw with Accrington that I watched with my family from the bare breeze-block away section at the Crown Ground, we had taken 25 points from our last 14 games – promotion form – and were on the edge of the play-off picture. But come January, like the season before, things started to go amiss.

Dwayne Mattis, the key driver of our engine room, was sold to Barnsley for £50,000. He wasn't the most popular member of the dressing room. He could be a bit spiky and aloof. Not easy to talk to. But one of the unwritten rules of the dressing room is that if you're important on the pitch, you can get away with almost anything. From being a bit spiky, like Mattis, to shagging a team-mate's missus (though I guess you need to be really important for that one). Players are very pragmatic like that. And we knew how much we would miss Dwayne.

We also got thrown out of the FA Cup for fielding an ineligible player in our replay win at Chester. I had to draft a letter to the board on behalf of the players to protest about us losing both the bonus money and the share of the gate receipts we would have been entitled to from the next round at Ipswich. The club came to an uneasy settlement with the squad, but Bish perhaps counted the biggest cost. With 15 goals to his name, he'd been rested ahead of an expected £250,000 move to, funnily enough, Ipswich. But when Chester were re-instated at our expense, Jon Walters took his opportunity to impress at Portman Road, and Ipswich signed him instead. The power of randomness once again.

Unable to replace the power and stature of Dwayne, our young midfield struggled to assert themselves. The goals started to dry up for Bish and Hursty. Well, for everyone really: we drew a blank in ten of 15 games between late January and mid-April. The loss of Kasper, back to parent club Manchester City and on to Falkirk, a month earlier also didn't help. He was definitely the best goalkeeper I played with. I think he made two errors that resulted in goals – and they weren't even obvious, glaring errors – in his 29 games for us over two seasons. He got fantastically upset one day in training when we were all winding him up about how many goals were going past him in a shooting drill. The truth was we were only over-egging it because he was practically unbeatable most of the time (well, that and the fact that he got so annoyed, it was funny!).

The upshot of all this was two wins in 20 post-Christmas games, and a fall from 9th to 21st, three points clear of the relegation places with three games to play, including daunting away trips to champions-elect Walsall and play-off chasing Stockport. For 13 of those 20 games, I was not in the matchday squad. I kept my head down in training, played the good professional with the kids in the reserves, scoring the odd goal, but I was the forgotten man. I still enjoyed coming in every day. There were people I liked spending time with in the dressing room, particularly Woodie, Brassy and Fetts. I still had the best job in the world. But it wasn't the same without a game to look forward to at the weekend.

Eventually, I think it was assistant Scotty, snapping after losing patience with Speighty, that persuaded the gaffer to bring me in from the cold. When I came on late in the two wins at Boston and Shrewsbury, I realised what my role had become. I was now the forward you brought on to hold on to a win. Not to get you a goal. Not to chase a result. But to keep what you had. In other words, a forward you brought on to improve your defence. Because, unlike a lot of attacking players, I would keep my concentration when we didn't have the ball; organising, dropping in when necessary to make it difficult for the opposition to dominate second balls and sustain pressure. As nice as it was to be back involved and making a contribution, it wasn't exactly a glamorous role. A role appreciated by others at the time, in those dying minutes, but not essential. Not the kind of player scouts would be beseeching their managers to sign at the end of the season, when it looked likely I would be a free agent again.

As we made the trip to Walsall – who'd just been confirmed

as promoted and were looking to celebrate in style – the chances of us being in front, and therefore requiring my skills as what they call a 'closer' in baseball, seemed remote. Walsall had the best home record in the division (we had the worst) and, in my former team-mates Martin Butler and Trevor Benjamin, had a front pairing I knew could hurt us. But as we got off the bus, Chris pulled me to one side. "I need you today," he said. "You're starting."

After a sum total of around 80 minutes of playing time in the previous six months, he suddenly 'needed' me for the biggest game of the season, away to the probable (and indeed eventual) champions, where defeat could help to consign Bury to non-League football after 113 years in the Football League. In most walks of life, to be asked to play such a crucial role with a couple of weeks left on your contract, having been basically deemed surplus to requirements for months, would be laughable. You'd tell them where to go and wish them well for the future. But football isn't most walks of life. You never know who might be watching. Aside from the potential of breaking my leg, I didn't have anything to lose. I was pretty sure I would be released anyway.

As Chris filled the changing room with the legendary Al Pacino pre-match speech from the American football film *Any Given Sunday*, I got my game head on. On a blisteringly hot day, we successfully frustrated the hosts early on and grew into the game. Three minutes before half-time, Jason Kennedy ('JK') hooked a hopeful ball forward. I read the bounce a bit better than Anthony 'cousin of Steven' Gerrard, and as he desperately tried to head clear, he could only knock the ball off my head and it deflected past Willy Gueret into the goal. 1-0. I was too honest about the exact nature of the goal with the press afterwards, as on the TV it doesn't look like that, it just looks like I beat him to the ball and headed it in. But it was a bit more fortuitous than that. It was still a goal, though. A very important goal. The travelling Bury fans even felt moved to sing my name for a few minutes. It was the first time I'd heard that since leaving Cambridge.

In the second half, no doubt roused by their manager Richard Money at the interval, Walsall put us under pressure. But we held out pretty comfortably, all told. They could point to Trev hitting a post and blazing a good chance over, but we also hit the post through JK and Will Mocquet came close as well. So on chances, they couldn't really argue with us meriting our unlikely win, which left us needing just one point to secure safety from our final two games. Of course, the obvious thing on my mind, as Chris gave me a hug at the final whistle, was 'so why, exactly, have I been left scratching my arse on matchdays for the last six months?' But it wasn't the time for that. I was just happy to feel useful again.

We got the point we needed to be mathematically safe at Stockport the following week, and then finished off with another draw, 1-1, at home to Mansfield. I scrambled home the equaliser from a corner, but by that stage I was pretty sure my days at the club were numbered. Keith Alexander, the former Peterborough and Lincoln boss who sadly died three years later, was in the stands amid rumours he would be coming in as director of football to help Chris. From playing against his ultra-direct Lincoln side, I didn't think I would be first in line for a new contract.

Like a year earlier, we were called in for meetings on the Monday. As I expected, I was informed of my release. Chris's exact words were: "I want to say thank you. You've saved us, really. But we need to make changes and I'm afraid that means you'll be moving on." Once the verdict was confirmed, I wasn't really up for small talk and quickly made my exit, only pausing to say goodbye to a couple of lads waiting to go in after me. Then I shot out of Gigg Lane for the last time.

League and cup appearances to this point
190 (+85 as sub), 56 goals

17

Too Proud for the Conference North?

I drove straight from my meeting to Staffordshire University. It was the intensive final week of the first year of my degree. I spoke to Brassy on the way down, who Bury had asked to come back for pre-season, with no guarantees beyond that. We both vented our frustrations, then he gave me the nod that our recently-departed goalkeeping coach, Ian Willcock, had put in a good word for me at his new club, Accrington, and that there might be something there for me. I'd also heard on the grapevine that Macclesfield, with boss Paul Ince having jumped ship to Milton Keynes, might be interested. I let Rich know both rumours so he could investigate.

For the rest of May I tried to switch off from the search for a club and concentrate on my degree. I was worried, of course. Being released by a club that had come pretty close to the bottom of the Football League two years on the bounce, and having not even held down a regular place there, was unlikely to make me anyone's prize capture that summer. But those two goals in the last three games gave me some hope, and Rich seemed confident, just as he had done before helping me sign for Bury. I trusted that he'd come through again. And I had plenty of university work to do. Stuff that might actually help me get a job when football had finally spat me out, whether that was the next week or in another ten years.

There was a shorthand exam to prepare for, a dissertation (or journalism project) to devise and start and a couple of weeks of work placement to do at Tower FM, the Bolton-based radio station for whom I'd done some co-commentaries when out in the cold (quite literally) at Gigg Lane. I'd already done plenty of hours on the sports desk at the *Bolton News* (which also produced the *Bury Times*) with Marc Iles. That was probably a bit more up my street than attending press conferences about changes to waste recycling initiatives and interviewing a local MP about an incentive to work programme. But it was all contributing to the end goal: a first-class degree. Something a bit more employer-friendly to put on a CV than 'once kicked a ball around for a living'.

In June, Chelle and I had a break back home visiting friends and family. Well, it had worked last time I was out of contract. This time I didn't get a call from Rich. I left him a couple of messages and thought I'd try again when we got back to Tottington. When we got there, I tried him again. And again. Finally, there was an answer. But it was Rich's wife, Jenny. He was seriously ill in hospital.

He'd had a heart bypass about a year or so before, and there had been complications in the aftermath, but since then he'd seemed ok. He'd come up and met me and Chelle for dinner. I'd spoken to him on a few occasions. The last one was only about two weeks previously. I'd had a couple of phone calls from clubs in the Conference North: Hyde and Southport. I asked Rich if I should at least agree to start pre-season training with one of them, unless he had any more news. He was adamant that he had some irons in the fire in the Football League, so I politely declined their offers.

When they'd called initially, an almost arrogant feeling of annoyance bubbled up inside me. Why would you target me? Why would you think I'm ready to drop two divisions outside the League? Do you think I'm done at that level, then? Foolish pride is what they call it, I think. Buoyed by Rich's confidence, I was probably a bit dismissive, though taking care not to offend or upset anyone.

But now Rich was out of action. And I still didn't have a club lined up. A sense of panic came over me after the phone call with Mrs Cody. I just wished I had known how ill he was, so I could have taken appropriate action.

Soon afterwards, I received a call from Jimmy Ball, son of Alan. Rich had represented Alan – who had recently passed away – over the years, so Jimmy wanted to help out any way he could. But he was, as he would confess, no agent. He followed up some leads Rich had scribbled down for him before becoming totally incapacitated. He called up people he knew within the game. Having drawn a blank with Morecambe and Accrington (who I'd seen had signed John Miles, a fellow PFA degree course student and a reasonably similar type of player to me), Jimmy thought he'd cracked it with his old friend Ian Brightwell, who'd succeeded Paul Ince at Macclesfield.

Chelle took the call while I was out on a run, trying to ensure I was ready to impress if I could find a club to train with. It was Tuesday and Jimmy had said that Ian, or someone from the club, would call me the next day with details of where to be for training on the Thursday. Macc – where Tippy had gone after falling out of favour at Bury – had staged a great escape from the bottom two after Ince took over in October with them seven points adrift. They were the only team to finish below Bury that didn't get relegated, and I doubted they would be fancied to finish much higher next time round. But they were still a full-time Football League side and I was in no position to be picky. If they were to give me a chance, I'd have to grasp it.

In the end, they were the ones who got picky. Scouring teletext at lunchtime on the day I was due to hear more from Macc, I saw that they had signed Michael Husbands, a young-ish striker from Port Vale. On a year's contract. I immediately wondered if my chance had gone. If that call would still arrive. It didn't. It's what they call the 'spinning plates' approach to recruitment: keep three or four possible signings interested, and work your way through them in order of preference if you miss out on your favoured option. I tried to call Jimmy and left him a message. He phoned back apologetically and said he was still trying to get hold of Ian. But I knew that was my last hope of staying in the League. Time to lower my sights and get out the contacts book.

In the meeting when Chris had informed me of my release,

he said he'd been contacted by Cambridge about me. As I was angry and didn't want to stick around any longer than absolutely necessary, I brushed it off with a curt "maybe". But in my head it wasn't a maybe. Aside from old adages about never going back to a club where you've had success, United were in freefall and had just come dangerously close to relegation to the Conference South. Which would have almost certainly meant oblivion, given the club's parlous financial state. At that point I didn't want to countenance going back to the Abbey. But now it was different. I was running out of options.

So on the Thursday morning I texted Chilli, the only senior player left from my time at the club, asking for manager Jimmy Quinn's number. While I waited for his reply, I went out for a run. Should have just stayed in and watched *Homes Under the Hammer*. If I had, I might soon have been back home, part of a newly-assembled Cambridge squad that would end up in the play-off final at Wembley that season. But I didn't.

I ran on a similar route to that which I'd covered many times before, down the footpath between Tottington village and the new estate that included our rental property. Towards the end of the path were some steps which led back up to the high street. I started to climb them but lost my footing, and as I tried to regain my balance I landed awkwardly and suddenly a feeling of fire shot through my calf. This was not like when I felt a sniper had targeted me against Luton a few years before. That was painful but this was on a different level. It felt more like someone had picked up my muscle and torn it in half, like you might with a baguette. I felt the muscle shred. I hobbled home uncomfortably and collapsed onto the sofa, close to tears.

Chelle fetched an ice pack, a Tubigrip and some ibuprofen. I heard Chilli's text reply come through. Fat lot of good it could do me now. I could just imagine the conversation: "Hello, Mr Quinn. You don't know me, but I'm well-thought of at the club – please could I have a contract? I won't be fit to play for at least a couple of months, but I'm sure that doesn't matter, does it? Forget all those other players who'll be able to train and play straight away. Oh, and you'll pay me in the meantime, yes?"

Looking back now, I probably still should have called, no matter how ridiculous it sounded in my head. I spoke to Jimmy a few years later and he confirmed that he had contacted Bury about trying to sign me. So he might have shown a bit of patience while I recovered. But I couldn't see it at the time. I just figured I should get myself fit and then start putting some feelers out. Apart from a couple of check-ups with the Bury physio, Alan Bent – who'd actually been the one to call me about going to Hyde, as he also worked for them – I looked after myself.

It was by far the worst muscle injury I'd ever had. After three weeks of icing and gently increasing my movements, I was still limping heavily. I had to force myself to start walking normally again, even though it was really painful to start with. To take my mind off the injury, I ploughed on with my studies. Once I'd been walking reasonably comfortably for a week or so, I started to do a bit of jogging. Gradually I built back up into full running, which I then started to develop into some fitness work, trying to compensate a little bit for all the pre-season I'd missed. The Football League season was already in full flow, four games in.

Out of the blue, Rich called me. I checked how he was doing and told him about the injury. "I can get you to Notts County for training, the week after next, so they can have a look at you," he said. "Are you fit enough for that?" One way to find out, I thought. I knew, though, deep down, that there would be nothing at County for me. Steve Thompson, their beleaguered manager, was an advocate of very direct football. He'd tried, unsuccessfully, to keep Cambridge in the League 18 months previously and was under severe pressure at Meadow Lane after a poor start to the campaign. I knew I wouldn't be his cup of tea, and he wouldn't be mine. This was just Rich calling on a friend to give me the illusion that he was still there to help me. But I knew he wasn't. It wasn't his fault; he was seriously ill. That was the last time I spoke to him. He sadly passed away the following year.

Irrespective of any incompatibility issues with Thompson, being a trialist didn't always suit me particularly well. As a player, I was more of a grower, like an album you love more with time. Not one jam-packed with catchy hit singles. I got a lovely letter from a Cambridge fan when I left the club, saying how he was sad to see me go. He reckoned I didn't always get the recognition I deserved from some fans because other players may have been more eye-catching. But he wanted to let me know he thought my lower-profile, under the radar work was really important for the team, and would be missed. That appreciation came having watched me over six years, though. In trials you don't get that long to make an impression. Eye-catching is what is needed.

If for nothing else, though, I could use the week at Notts to regain a bit of fitness. And catch up with some old friends. Lawrie Dudfield, Adam Tann and Neil Mackenzie were all there. Macca invited me to stay at his newly-purchased flat in the city centre. I think he wanted the company. He'd only opted to join Notts thanks to a last-minute U-turn on a train to Darlington, with whom he'd practically agreed terms. He was now regretting that change of heart. Hugely. He didn't like Thompson at all, a fact that came as no surprise to me. I did my best to keep his spirits up before the assistant manager, John Gannon, told me what I already knew – that there were no prospects for me at the club – after training on the Friday.

That night I gave Freddie Murray, my erstwhile team-mate at Cambridge and Northampton, a call. He'd rung me earlier in the summer, while I was injured, as he was on trial at Accrington and knew I lived up that way. He offered to get me involved in a trial game at Stanley, at which point I had to confess that I wasn't fit enough to play, even if they'd have me. With nothing forthcoming at Accrington, he'd signed a short-term deal at Stafford Rangers in the Conference. "I've gotta get you down here," he said, his quickly-spoken Irish accent conveying an urgency quite apt for the situation. "I'll have a word with the gaffer at the game tomorrow."

Tomorrow was the day the removal van was coming to take all our things into storage. Having sold the house (just in time – the credit crunch hit within a couple of months), we passed the keys on to its new owners. Chelle and I would live back at

Mum's until we could sort out a house to rent, whether that was back home in Suffolk or near a new club.

Stafford boss Phil Robinson, the former Wolves midfielder, invited me to train on the Monday. On the face of it, it seemed promising. I was at uni down the road in Stoke one or two days a week, so it would be a very convenient base if I could land a contract. Initially, I signed on non-contract terms. "I'll make sure you clear £250 a week after tax," Phil said. I was straight into the side for the trip to York, one of the division's bigger spenders, the following evening. I just about managed to get through a tough 90 minutes on the right wing. Despite my lack of fitness, it was a real buzz to be back out on the pitch. But there was no hiding that I was struggling to keep pace with the game. A few cross-country runs and a week's training at Notts County were not exactly equivalent to a good pre-season. So I was on the bench for the next few matches as I tried to build both base fitness and football sharpness in training, and a reserve match at Tamworth, where I managed to net a well-taken goal. The sessions put on by Phil and assistant David Oldfield were excellent and enjoyable. The matches, however, were not.

Whether playing a part or just watching, it was painful to see a largely young Stafford side trying manfully to compete in a division in which they were out of their depth, eventually losing 33 of 46 games. They were a willing, honest set of lads, and Phil was a clever and enthusiastic coach, but against the likes of Cambridge, Oxford, Torquay, Exeter and Stevenage, it was almost impossible for Stafford to measure up. Particularly as the already miniscule budget – with which Phil had somehow avoided relegation by a narrow margin the previous season – had been cut drastically at the start of the campaign.

After six weeks with the club, and finally starting to look fit, I approached Phil with a bit of an ultimatum. I required something more concrete than a non-contract deal if I was going to be able to rent a house somewhere nearby. I'd spent a lot of money since being at the club: driving the 290-mile round trip from Mildenhall three or four times a week; staying in a hotel after my uni evenings so I could get to training the following morning. I couldn't keep doing that, so I told him I needed a contract. Just six months until the end of the season would enable me to move up to the area, I thought.

Phil called me as I sat in a launderette in Stafford, waiting for my training kit to dry (very glamorous, I know!). Nothing doing. I wasn't overly surprised. I think, subconsciously, I'd made the request knowing it would be turned down, forcing me to look elsewhere. I couldn't see myself being able to function well in a team with so little possession, so little quality, fighting desperate rearguard actions every week. They needed midfield scrappers. Forwards or widemen with pace and power, to make the most of the isolated opportunities to break they would engineer. I didn't fit the brief. As much as I respected Phil and wished nothing but the best for the boys, I didn't think my sticking around would help them very much, and it certainly wouldn't be much fun for me. My departure was swiftly followed by that of David Oldfield, a host of other non-contract players, and, a few weeks later, by Phil, who'd enjoyed six successful years in charge. The embattled, financially-stricken club were starting the downward spiral that would see them plummet three divisions in seven years.

On the way home from Stafford, I called Peter Davenport. The ex-Manchester United and Nottingham Forest striker was the Southport manager who'd phoned me twice over the summer, trying to get me over to Merseyside. Whereas Stafford were consigned to peril at the bottom of the Conference, Southport – a club with proud Football League traditions – were in contention for promotion from the Conference North. For two weeks running, I went up for a couple of days' training after uni. Chelle and I stayed in the grand old Scarisbrick hotel on the seafront, where we watched England fail to qualify for the 2008 European Championships on 'wally with a brolly' night.

I liked the town. The squad was talented. Peter and his coach Huw Griffiths spoke well. And they seemed impressed with me. Chelle even started scouting for possible rental homes in the area, so we could move quickly if the need arose. It didn't. Peter seemed really keen to sign me on a deal worth about

£300 a week, but couldn't get the chairman to commit to more than a month-to-month contract. As I was currently living 220 miles away, that wasn't really an option. I'd spent quite enough money on petrol and hotel stays in the past two months. Our savings had been plundered. It was back to square one.

Almost as soon as I got home, my brother had a message for me. Steve O'Donohue, director of football at Cambridge City, the Conference South side, had enquired about what I was doing. "Tell him we'd always have room for him here," was the message. I called him back and after meeting boss Gary Roberts and the squad at training on the Thursday, I was in the squad for the four-hour trip to Newport. It ended up a wasted journey, torrential rain in South Wales seeing the game postponed soon after our arrival. But in the clubhouse at Newport, I agreed non-contract terms of £220 a week with Gary. As it was a 25-minute drive to the ground for either training or games, the terms were a lot more financially viable than at Stafford or Southport, even though the weekly wage was lower.

At home, Chelle was able to get her old job back at RAF Lakenheath. We started renting a place and got all our things back from storage. I landed another two-week work placement, at the *Cambridge Evening News*, where I knew some of the lads and felt at home. Suddenly, having lived a nomadic existence riddled with uncertainty for a few months, we felt settled again. But, annoyingly, I didn't get much of a chance to settle in at Cambridge City.

After a few appearances from the bench and two from the start – and a couple of goals to boot – I was on the bench for the FA Trophy tie at Conference Premier Droylsden. Coming on after an hour on a boggy pitch in cold conditions, I looked pretty sharp for 15 minutes but, as I tried to shield the ball from a defender clambering all over me, I felt my hamstring pull. My over-zealous marker had effectively doubled the weight my legs were having to support for a few seconds, and, with no pre-season and precious little football under my belt in recent months, my unconditioned hammy couldn't take the strain.

Under the experienced, watchful eye of physio Joe Miller,

I eased back into training and, after coming through three sessions unscathed, got back into the squad for our visit to Havant & Waterlooville. Summoned to enter the fray 20 minutes from time, with us trailing 2-1, I lasted about five minutes. On another mud-heap, I turned to sprint in the Havant half and, similar to my calf the previous summer, felt my muscle shred. As Joe and one of the other subs supported me on a painful stagger back to the dugout, I knew my season was over. It was February 9th; even if I managed to get training again within six weeks – which seemed a long shot given how long the calf recovery had taken – I'd have to build up fitness again to even think about getting through a match. By then, there would be hardly any games left. Gary took me to one side, thanked me for my efforts and said I'd be welcome back for pre-season, but he'd have to terminate my deal.

And so ended my first season outside the Football League. Before it had ever got started. I would have hoped, if unable to secure a move within the League, to find somewhere suitable to get some games, score some goals and hopefully put myself back in the shop window. But events had conspired to make it a soul-crushing blur of injuries, fruitless trial periods and nights in hotels. The best thing to come out of it was Chelle and I getting to add to our collection of Pizza Express locations visited. Not a great year, then.

But I still had a chance to drag something positive out of the most difficult 12 months of my adult life thus far. In no shape to play football, I could concentrate on finishing my degree as strongly as possible. I undertook another three work placements, leaning on previous football contacts to get a foot in the door at BBC Radio Cambridgeshire, the *East Anglian Daily Times* and the *Northampton Chronicle & Echo*. I'd secured a weekly column in the newspaper *Non-League Today* to fulfil the requirements of my journalism project, and ended up doing more and more work for them. Having finally completed and submitted all the necessary work, I could relax in the knowledge that I'd shown my best.

When the results came in later that summer, I had what I

wanted. A first-class degree with honours. I spoke to my class-mates, former Chelsea left-back Scott Minto and ex-Rotherham stalwart (and future Grimsby Town manager) Paul Hurst, who'd also done well, to offer reciprocated congratulations. Other fellow graduates included ex-Sheffield Wednesday captain Lee Bullen, former England under-21 international Adi Moses and my old team-mate at Bury, Smarty. One mission accomplished, it was time to re-focus on trying to salvage my football career.

Using my guise as a reporter for *Non-League Today*, I got some numbers to target some old acquaintances. John Dreyer, my former Cambridge team-mate (known to all in the game as 'Tumble' – geddit!) had just pitched up at Stevenage as No 2 to the returning Graham Westley. We had a good catch-up and he invited me to pre-season at Broadhall Way. Having continued to visit Joe at Cambridge City to monitor my hamstring, I'd made sure I was fully fit when late June rolled around. By the time I arrived, though, Graham had already set about building a title-challenging side, signing a glut of new faces, including a few strikers (to go with Steve Morison, my old team-mate who'd already blossomed into one of the division's most feared frontmen). With each new addition that I saw come through on the club website over the summer, my chances of landing a deal got slimmer.

But I still gave it everything I had, and enjoyed a good two weeks, including half an hour in a friendly win at Gillingham. Graham, though admittedly a bit eccentric (singing a Bon Jovi song as part of a team-talk is only ever going to invite ridicule!), was nothing like the unstable fruitcake I'd expected from a host of message board rumours and Chinese whispers from players. He put on good, meaningful sessions, was detailed in his preparations and gave clear instructions. I wasn't at all surprised to see him take Stevenage from strength to strength. Eventually, Tumble pulled me aside for the expected 'thanks, but no thanks' chat, offering a few kind words, and it was on to my next target.

Paul Carden, the Cambridge captain, had known me briefly from Bury when he came on trial there. He'd just been promoted to player-assistant manager under his friend, the surprise appointment, Gary Brabin. Calling Cardy for an interview, I thought (well, hoped) he might get curious and ask what I was doing. He did. And so came another invitation to train.

We trained at yet another of the beautiful college grounds in the city, not one I'd been to before. So it wasn't quite like coming home. But there was something reassuringly familiar about it all. And I trained really well. But my problem was that already established at the club, having had a good season as United made the Wembley play-off final in 2008, was Mark Beesley. A centre-forward with a neat touch, who liked to come short and link play, but couldn't run away from anyone. Words that could just as easily apply to me. In a couple of runouts against local non-League sides, I was tried in various midfield positions and only got a couple of short spells as a striker. I didn't set the world alight. Didn't even get it particularly warm. No matter how well I was doing in training, I could feel the writing starting to appear on the wall.

At the very least I was promised I'd get back on the Abbey, against a youthful West Ham side. I came on at half-time, partnering the giant Lee McEvilly in attack. Whereas in the earlier, low-key friendlies I could almost feel the pressure grow with every minute in which I didn't do anything memorable or creative, getting back out in front of the Cambridge faithful made all the pressure vanish. If it was to prove a swansong, so be it. But I was going to enjoy myself. And I played really well. I was on the ball constantly, slipping perceptive passes through gaps and creating chances. It would have been nice to have a chance to score, but at least I'd had one last hurrah playing towards the Newmarket Road end.

After another week, I spoke to Gary in the bar after our final game at Braintree was postponed due to a rutted surface. "I saw something in that West Ham game," he said. "After the other games, I was saying to Cardy: 'He's not a midfielder, he's not a winger, not for me'. But I saw something I liked in the West Ham game. Here's the thing, though. I don't need a forward who fronts up and comes into pockets. I've got Bees for that.

I need what I haven't got. Someone who goes the other way." Within a couple of days, in came Chris Holroyd from Chester to provide just that.

Cardy tried to set me up with Conference South Braintree, where I trained one evening before I received a call from my former Cambridge City team-mate, Ben Bowditch. He persuaded his boss at St Albans City, former Peterborough midfielder Steve Castle, to bring me in. I agreed to be on the bench for their opening game of the season at home to Havant. For five winless games, I made brief contributions as a sub, but I was struggling to find any enjoyment.

I was driving for an hour and 20 minutes each way on a Tuesday and Thursday evening, having been on the phone all day chasing stories for the paper, and when I got there it was just so far removed from what I had been used to as a full-time professional. Steve, and his assistant Andy Edwards, were former pros and tried to make sure the sessions had definite objectives and everything was done to a good standard. And the lads, many who'd had some grounding within the pro game, were decent enough players and never short on effort. But, having come from their day jobs, I felt the sessions were as much a release for them as a place to be completely focused. The odd session would deteriorate into grumbling, moaning and apathy. And a loss of quality.

It had been similar, at times, at Cambridge City. Again, that was no particular fault of the manager or squad. It was unfair to compare it to the pro game, but I couldn't shake the feeling of being second-rate.

I don't mean, in any way, to denigrate non-League, or grassroots football. Lots of players, many far better than me, have emerged from non-League into the pro game. Some even to the very top (Ian Wright, Stuart Pearce, Jamie Vardy and many more). Grassroots is the lifeblood of the sport. It rightly plays an important part in many people's lives, and went on to do so in mine. That second-rate feeling was just my personal, gut reaction to knowing I would never return to the professional ranks.

My physical decline, which was becoming more marked at the grand old age of 29, was not helping either. The lack of full-time training, which had probably helped to ward off problems by keeping me as fit as possible over the years, may have been key. It was almost as if I was seizing up and slowing down with every evening session. Only two years later, with the severity of my arthritis laid bare, could I come to appreciate why.

When Steve called to say he needed to save my money on the budget to re-invest in the defence, I was relieved. I'd come to the realisation that if my time in the professional game was over – which it clearly was – I shouldn't fixate on playing at the highest level possible, when it could never re-create the fulfilment of being a pro. Especially when I was doing a 140-mile round trip, three times a week to bring in £100 a game.

So I decided to finally give in to Dave Pinkowski, the manager of Mildenhall Town, who'd been chasing me for over a year. It's not like I could escape him easily; he lived three doors down.

**League and cup appearances (final – nothing to add!)
190 (+85 as sub), 56 goals**

18

Entering Injury Time

My initial return to Mildenhall, a semi-pro outfit in the Eastern Counties League, Premier Division, started well enough but descended into a bit of shambles. Disputes over money, players and managers leaving in acrimonious circumstances, it became like a soap opera. And I've never been a fan of those. I even ended up in caretaker charge for eight games or so, struggling to get a team out on the pitch at Dereham when a couple of players got lost en route via a visit to the bookies.

Short spells at Norwich United and Newmarket Town in the same league didn't help me regain any sense of footballing purpose. Since leaving the full-time game, I had been a ball of frustration, struggling to deal with the comedown in terms of attitude and approach, both from some of the players and also some of the managers that I couldn't find much common ground with. I'd been troubled by back and hip complaints as well, that were seriously compromising my ability to show anything like the class expected of a player with over 250 Football League games playing five divisions below League Two. By July 2010, I was seriously contemplating giving up football altogether.

Then came a phone call from the newly-appointed manager of Mildenhall, Christian Appleford. I agreed to meet up for a chat, where he asked me to be player-assistant manager for the new season. I wasn't really prepared for that. I'd never taken my coaching badges because I never wanted to be a coach or manager. Too many ex-players, too few jobs, and a complete lack of job security even if you're lucky enough to find a role. Helping kids to learn the game held an appeal, but I don't think coaches at that level are valued highly enough in this country to make it a bankable way to support a family.

This offer wouldn't mean I was committing to a new career in the game, though. It was a low-key, part-time role. Christian was a highly-qualified coach who wanted to take all the training sessions. He just needed me to provide a sounding board, an alternative opinion and to help him spot where games were being won or lost on a Saturday. The two main bugbears driving me to despair over the past couple of years had been that: a) training was often not useful, relevant or worth everyone's time; and b) match-day preparation was poor and haphazard. This seemed the perfect opportunity to have an input to those issues and create an environment which didn't make me want to quit playing football.

It worked. We had a really enjoyable first season, finishing fifth in the league and lifting the Cambs FA Invitation Cup at the Abbey. After battling through some early injury problems, I managed to play over 30 games, even finding myself often in the central midfield role I probably should have targeted many years previously when the chance first arose at Cambridge. Excusing one or two games of, ahem, Wembley doubles, training remained a worthwhile endeavour. And I felt I was adding value by imparting my experience and understanding, particularly on match-days. Football was making me happy again.

This was a striking contrast from just over two years previously, when I'd first dropped down to Step Five level. Though on the pitch things had started well, gradually two factors combined to leave me feeling very low.

The aforementioned disillusionment with standards underlined just how far I'd fallen, and brought into focus how much I missed being a full-time footballer. And being able to call myself a full-time footballer. Stories are legion of footballers unable to adapt to life after the professional ranks, and I was definitely starting to feel somewhat deflated. My self-esteem was wounded.

Alongside that was a realisation that the new career path I'd headed down was perhaps not really what I wanted. In a bit of a whirlwind, I'd thrown myself into a degree that really interested me, before – while going through the drawn out end of one career – jumping straight into a new job freelancing for *Non-League Today*. Without even pausing for thought. It seemed a natural transition, combining a love of football and a love of writing. But over the coming months I found that a love of writing did not translate into a love of journalism.

My major issue was in not being able to put my work down. The phone was always on; there were always plenty of messages I'd left with people that could be returned at any time, day or night. I felt I had to be constantly on the blower, cycling through all the people I knew in the game. I was living in fear of missing a major story, of not having made the one phone call that could have led to something big. I couldn't switch off from it all, and I never felt satisfied with my work. I was struggling to sleep. And this was just writing for a minor publication. I could only imagine it swamping me even more were I to move further up the food chain. Lots of great journalists live for that thrill of chasing a story, claiming a scoop. Of ruffling people's feathers to generate a reaction, and with it fresh copy. And it's a fantastic job for them. It just wasn't for me. While I lived for my features, where I could craft a longer, more interesting piece, utilising a bit more creativity, I didn't feel cut out for the job as a whole.

Finally, it all – the footballing downgrade and journalistic struggles – got on top of me. I was suffering anxiety and panic attacks and a cloud grew above me. I phoned Chelle at work one day to talk about something completely unrelated, but broke down. She – pregnant with our first child and in no need of such drama – rushed home to support me. I phoned my very understanding boss at *Non-League Today*, Dave Watters. He recognised my symptoms as similar to a friend of his who was battling depression, so wanted to help any way he could. He agreed to shrink my workload but keep me on board. I resolved to keep playing football, at least for the time being, to bring in a bit of money while I pondered my next move. I needed a new plan.

Unlike many who long to exit the rat race, I wanted in. I was craving a nine-to-five existence, something reliable to pay the bills but that could be set aside more easily at the end of the day. Working hard wasn't a problem, I'd always done that. I just wanted that work to have more definite boundaries.

To that end, I put myself through the first part of the AAT accounting qualification. Aside from writing, my other biggest strengths academically were maths and logic, and I had friends who worked in accountancy. It felt like a pretty stable, reliable career to aim for, certainly compared to football and journalism. Having spoken to a couple of recruitment agencies, I got the course completed and exams passed before putting myself on the market for potential employers. By a stroke of good fortune, within two days I'd been placed in a temporary role at brewing and pub company, Greene King, in nearby Bury St Edmunds. And by a further slice of luck, a resignation opened up the chance of a permanent contract six weeks later. My new career was up and running. Coinciding with the optimism of my fresh start at Mildenhall, and the first year of my first daughter Hannah's life, the cloud above me had cleared.

But there was a new cloud on the horizon. It was just a few weeks into my second season under Christian that the fateful fall on my left hip came. At least I could say my final football match was a 9-0 win, even if I only played for about 15 minutes of it. Wisbech did help by getting three men sent off by the hour mark. What became my last goal had come ten days previously, a stooping – so low I nearly butted the floor on the follow-through – stoppage-time header to seal three points at Wivenhoe.

It was three weeks before I could shake off a heavy limp. I was getting out of the office chair like a creaking old man. When the specialist Mr Parsons saw my x-rays, he said: "Blimey! What painkillers are you on?" "None," I said. The cartilage in my hip was so calcified it was more like bone than soft tissue. So what would have been a labral tear was more like a fracture. It was not going to heal, only get worse. More surprisingly, he said that if he'd been shown my x-rays without having spoken to me, he would have assumed my right hip was the problem, not my left. The angle and shape of my femur head entering the socket were all wrong and he struggled to believe I wasn't having further issues on that side.

That was quite instructive of events earlier in my career. I had major problems with flexibility in my teens and early twenties. I devoted lots of time to stretching my hamstrings, and over time I did see improvement. This helped to protect my muscles, and I can only remember having two minor hamstring strains during my ten-year professional career – one the day I scored my first League goal and one when I was at Orient. "Bloody hell, I thought you had to have pace to pull a hamstring!" Lingy joked.

But my groins were a different matter. I was always getting niggles in them. I tried to stretch them just as much as my hammies, but never made any headway. "I treat arthritic grannies with more flexibility than you," laughed Stuart Ayles once when trying to treat my tweaked groin. Little did we know how appropriate that comparison was. As Mr Parsons said: "This situation started long before you were born. Your hips developed in this way and it means they've been poorly equipped to handle life, particularly when put through the constant trauma of football." It wasn't tight groin muscles preventing my flexibility, not principally. It was balls and sockets that had grown in an incompatible way, so were unable to provide the normal pivots expected of the joint. I was never able to volley the ball on the side because I couldn't get my leg over the ball. Now I knew why.

Mr Parsons said that he knew other specialists that, thanks to the private medical insurance provided by my job, would happily recommend a couple of expensive, less invasive procedures than outright replacement. He insisted he would have no issue with me seeking a second opinion, but that he genuinely believed it would be a waste of time and have no real effect. We were past the stage of minor correction. As I seemed to be dealing pretty well with the pain, he was happy to leave it up to me regarding the need for surgery. "Come back when you can't take it anymore," he said.

I'm not there yet. It's important that I delay it as long as possible because hip replacements don't last indefinitely. Current expectancy is around 25-30 years. Which is fine given the ages most people have the operation. But not if you have it done earlier. Ideally I don't want to risk going through what is a major procedure, with all the accompanying risks, as many as four times (if I ended up needing to replace each hip twice). So I've just been very careful since. Apart from once, when I allowed myself to be drawn into a tug of war at a team bonding day at work. It didn't immediately occur to me that it would cause me a problem. Not clever. For the rest of the week, I could only lift my left leg by actually picking it up with my hands and moving it where I needed. Putting on socks and shoes was not much fun. At least no one was there to watch.

After my meeting with Mr Parsons, obviously my playing days were over. But I really wanted to stay on as Christian's assistant. Thankfully, he was happy to have me. I knew that not being able to play was going to hit me hard, and I figured that still being involved, analysing the game and offering my opinions, would be a good way to wean me off football slowly. So that I could eventually free up my weekends for family life, as the girls – Hannah soon to be joined by sister Orla – grew up.

For a good few months, having lost the release of playing, I was an angry little man. I'm sure Chelle took the brunt of it at home, but referees were taking more than their fair share of my wrath on match-days. It was only when one ref, at Gorleston, looked at me almost pityingly as I completely blew my top, that I realised I needed to have a good look in the mirror. It was over a throw-in. Five yards from the halfway line, for goodness sake. As his withering glare registered, I felt quite pathetic. Having recognised that being unable to play was driving my rage, and knowing that situation wasn't ever going to change, I made a conscious decision from that point on to do the proverbial count to ten whenever I felt things bubbling up. I think it's worked, but I guess you'd have to ask my wife. Coincidentally, it was back at Gorleston about 18 months later that I first experienced problems with my vision.

I was struggling to follow the game, only knowing we'd

opened the scoring because I heard the cheers of the boys and our small but merry band of supporters. I put it down to suffering from a heavy cold while a low, bright sun hovered over the stands. But the following week at work brought no relief and so began the series of tests that led to my MS diagnosis. And, eventually, the end of my time in football.

It was certainly the right decision to walk away from the game. The three years since my injury had shown me clearly just how all-consuming the management side of things can be. It's far more involved than being a player, when you pretty much just turn up, train or play, then go home. Of course I used to think about the games and analyse my own performances, but it was easier to dispel it from your mind. As part of the management, you're constantly thinking about the team.

Where are things going well? Where are they not? How can we improve this in training? Who's in form? Who's not? Could we try a different system (we always worked on a few different formations, as we believed changing shape during a match could be far more effective to alter a game's dynamic than merely changing personnel)? Are there any players available to improve us? What do I know about our opponents? What more can I find out? What threats do they pose and how can we deal with them? What weaknesses do they have and how do we target them? I'd be in touch with Christian regularly outside of training and match-days. When my phone rang, my daughters used to say, automatically, "is it Christian?" Mostly it was. And while I really enjoyed the research, the analysis, the planning, coming on top of the day job and family life – or more specifically a one-year-old specialising in broken sleep – it wasn't helping me get any less tired.

Even since stepping away from football, I get very tired. My visual issues have remained constant, leading to bouts of disorientation and exacerbating my feelings of fatigue. I've become acutely susceptible to Uhtoff's phenomenon, a complication of MS whereby increased body temperature worsens symptoms, particularly vision as the damaged optic nerve cannot handle it. Even just walking on a warm day, or having hot soup for lunch, can make my eyesight go completely haywire. I have to keep my showers short and can't have a bath or I'll feel lousy for some time afterwards. It would be a problem when it comes to keeping fit, if it wasn't for my hips meaning the only way I can exercise pain-free is by swimming, which mercifully comes with an in-built cooling environment.

It was strange getting back into swimming at the age of 32. I was an avid swimmer as a youngster, before football took over my world. But having rarely been in the pool other than for warm-downs since, I found that I was no longer a great shape for it. As a footballer, your power and bulk tends to get concentrated in your thighs and bum. In the pool, this just means your bottom half sinks. It's hard work to keep horizontal. When I first started up again, I could manage two lengths at most before needing to take a short break. A little bit embarrassing when the average age of those effortlessly cruising up and down around you is over 60. But I kept at it and within six months I could be straight out of bed, down to the pool and rattle off half a mile in time to get home for breakfast and then on to work. It keeps me reasonably fit, though a million miles, of course, from where I used to be.

I still feel on top of my MS at the moment, and long may that continue. I haven't been too keen to talk about it with people, mainly because the words "multiple sclerosis" sound horrific when said aloud, and drive extreme reactions. Mum looked pretty horrified when I first told her. And as most people aren't too aware of what MS actually is and does – like I wasn't, initially – I didn't want anyone to start looking at me differently. But I realised that it's important to be open about it, to raise awareness and prevent those over-reactions. So I thought I'd write this book.

MS causes the body's immune system to attack its nervous system, through the process of demyelination. Which means that myelin, the coating which protects nerves and helps them to transmit signals correctly around the body, gets stripped away. So the nerves get damaged and don't work properly. And as this damage can affect any part of the body, people get vastly different symptoms, and varying degrees of them. Hence why MS can be totally different from person to person.

Reading up on the many theories about the still largely opaque causes of the condition (well, if I'm honest, Chelle's been the real driving force behind that), I've tried to do my bit by improving my diet. I eat less meat (which Chelle being a vegan makes easier) and have reduced my dairy intake. I've mostly cut out caffeine. Decaf all the way for tea and coffee and Coke has been banned from the house (though it's still a vice I occasionally submit to when out). I've stopped drinking. I was never a big drinker anyway, and my body does disorientated and wobbly well enough on its own at times now. I don't need to give it any further encouragement through alcohol. These are small sacrifices that may or may not really help me, but they're worth a shot to help ward off the optic neuritis, the fatigue, the dips in concentration and any other potential symptoms. To ensure I can keep functioning at work and support my family. And keep playing a full and active role in their life.

I tend to view my condition in moderate terms. It's not ideal. It would be better if I didn't have it. But while relapsing-remitting MS is a potentially serious condition, it's a manageable one. Things could be much worse. It's similar to how I look back on my football career. It could have been better. It's not quite what dreams are made of. I didn't play for England, or in the Premier League. Heck, I'm not even be the most famous sportsman with my own name anymore, thanks to my rugby-playing namesake with his stash of international caps. But it could have been a whole lot worse. I'm lucky to have played so many times as a professional, and scored more than a few goals. Despite some low-points, particularly in the last few chapters, this is no sob story.

I continue to feel lucky. I may still drive a shed, but I have a wonderful family and friends. I'm not going to let MS get in the way of that, if I can help it. And if it's a bit of resilience I need, that's just one more reason to be thankful for a football career which means I've got plenty. One of my stock lines in job interviews, when they ask what I'm like under pressure, is:

"Well, I'm used to an environment where one mistake can lead to a few thousand people calling you every name under the sun at deafening volume, so I hope I can handle whatever this job can throw at me."

And I hope I can be more than a match for anything MS may have in store.